Home Library

EDITOR: Maryanne Blacker

FOOD EDITOR: Pamela Clark

• • •

ART DIRECTOR: Paula Wooller

DESIGNER: Robbylee Phelan

SUB-EDITOR: Mary-Anne Danaher

• • •

DEPUTY FOOD EDITOR: Jan Castorina

ASSISTANT FOOD EDITOR: Kathy Snowball

ASSOCIATE FOOD EDITOR: Enid Morrison

SENIOR HOME ECONOMISTS: Alexandra McCowan, Louise Patniotis, Kathy Wharton

HOME ECONOMISTS: Cynthia Black, Leisel Chen, Kathy McGarry, Tracey Port, Maggie Quickenden, Dimitra Stais

EDITORIAL COORDINATOR: Elizabeth Hooper

KITCHEN ASSISTANT: Amy Wong

• • •

STYLISTS: Lucy Andrews, Marie-Helene Clauzon, Carolyn Fienberg, Jane Hann, Rosemary de Santis

PHOTOGRAPHERS: Kevin Brown, Robert Clark, Tim Cole, Cath Muscat, Robert Taylor, Jon Waddy

• • •

HOME LIBRARY STAFF

ASSISTANT EDITOR: Beverley Hudec

EDITORIAL COORDINATOR: Fiona Nicholas

• • •

PUBLISHER: Richard Walsh

ASSOCIATE PUBLISHER: Bob Neil

• • •

Produced by The Australian Women's Weekly Home Library.
Typeset by ACP Colour Graphics Pty Ltd. Printed by Dai Nippon Co., Ltd in Japan.
Published by ACP Publishing Pty Ltd, 54 Park Street, Sydney.
♦ AUSTRALIA: Distributed by Network Distribution Company, 54 Park Street Sydney, (02) 282 8777.
♦ UNITED KINGDOM: Distributed in the U.K. by Australian Consolidated Press (UK) Ltd, 20 Galowhill Rd, Brackmills, Northampton NN4 OEE (0604) 760 456.
♦ CANADA: Distributed in Canada by Whitecap Books Ltd, 1086 West 3rd St, North Vancouver V7P 3J6 (604) 980 9852.
♦ NEW ZEALAND: Distributed in New Zealand by Netlink Distribution Company, 17B Hargreaves St, Level 5, College Hill, Auckland 1 (9) 302 7616.
♦ SOUTH AFRICA: Distributed in South Africa by Intermag, PO Box 57394, Springfield 2137 (011) 493 3200.
ACN 053 273 546

• • •

Easy Greek-Style Cookbook

Includes index.
ISBN 1 86396 000 7.

1. Cookery. 2. Entertaining. (Series: Australian Women's Weekly Home Library).

641.5'68

• • •

• • •

COVER: Clockwise from back: Roast Garlic Lamb with Lemon Potatoes, page 92; Mushroom Fillo Triangles, page 17; Vine Leaves with Pine Nuts and Currants, page 13. Centre: Taramosalata, page 2.
Platter, jars, white bowl and small plates from Country Floors; large plate from Country Road Homewear.
OPPOSITE: Beetroot Salad with Garlic Sauce, page 29.
BACK COVER: Almond Pears, page 118.
WE WOULD LIKE TO THANK RINNAI FOR THE GAS BURNER USED IN THE STEPS IN THIS BOOK.

Easy GREEK-STYLE *Cookery*

Right now, you can start a fascinating journey to Greece with this book. Your passport is our step-by-step recipes where you cook, taste and learn the secrets of Greek-style home cooking. Freshness of ingredients is all-important, with lemons, garlic, olive oil, herbs and spices adding authentic flavours. It is hearty food, great to share with warmth, friendliness and hospitality as you would in Greece. With a meal, put plenty of bread, olives and wine on the table, then linger over it all, with coffee and sweets later. Sometimes, recipes and names vary between regions, but we give you favourites that are delicious under any name.

Pamela Clark

FOOD EDITOR

BRITISH & NORTH AMERICAN READERS: Please note that Australian cup and spoon measurements are metric. A Quick Conversion Guide appears on page 127.
A glossary explaining unfamiliar terms and ingredients appears on page 124.

APPETISERS & SOUPS

MEZETHES KE SOUPES

A delicious way to share hospitality is by offering mezethes, or "little bits", when friends meet or visitors call. We've made favourites from an enormous variety, and you can serve just one or more, up to a lavish spread before a celebration. With mezethes, it is usual to serve drinks, but alcohol is never served without food. Soups, too, are popular, and important as starters or as hearty meals.

TARAMOSALATA WITH ARTICHOKES

Taramosalata me Anginares

4 slices stale white bread
100g tarama (salted fish roe)
½ small onion, grated
1 small clove garlic, crushed
¼ cup (60ml) lemon juice
⅔ cup (160ml) olive oil
6 small fresh globe artichokes

1. Remove crusts from bread, soak bread in cold water 2 minutes. Drain, squeeze water from bread.

2. Blend or process bread, tarama, onion, garlic and juice until well combined and creamy. While motor is operating, gradually add oil in a thin stream; process until well combined. Serve taramosalata in artichoke hearts; as a dip with artichoke leaves and bread, or as an accompaniment to Greek meals.

3. Trim base of artichokes so they sit flat. Remove any tough outer leaves and trim remaining leaves with scissors. Rinse artichokes under cold water. Add artichokes to pan of boiling water, boil, uncovered, about 30 minutes or until artichoke hearts are tender when pricked with a fork; drain, rinse under cold water.

4. Open artichokes slightly and carefully remove the inner soft leaves and hairy choke with a teaspoon.

Serves 6.

- Taramosalata can be made a week ahead.
- Storage: Covered, in refrigerator.
- Freeze: Not suitable.
- Microwave: Artichokes suitable.

Pot from Corso de Fiori; fabric from Les Olivades.

SEAFOOD SOUP

Kakavia

300g medium uncooked prawns
1 small (about 200g) lobster tail
1.2kg fish heads and bones
1 large onion, chopped
1 stick celery, chopped
1 medium carrot, chopped
2 bay leaves
8 sprigs fresh lemon thyme
2 litres (8 cups) water
2 tablespoons olive oil
1 large leek, sliced
3 cloves garlic, thinly sliced
1 stick celery, chopped, extra
3 medium tomatoes, peeled,
    seeded, chopped
1½ tablespoons chopped fresh
    lemon thyme
½ cup (125ml) dry white wine
¼ cup (60ml) tomato paste
½ teaspoon fennel seeds
1 large potato, chopped
1 teaspoon sugar
salt, pepper
250g firm white fish fillets
150g scallops
2 tablespoons chopped fresh parsley
¼ cup (60ml) lemon juice

2. Heat oil in pan, add leek and garlic, cook, stirring, until leek is soft. Add extra celery, tomatoes, chopped lemon thyme and wine, boil, uncovered, until vegetables are soft.

3. Stir in combined stock, paste and seeds, simmer, uncovered, 10 minutes. Add potato, simmer about 5 minutes or until potato is just tender; add sugar and salt and pepper to taste.

1. Shell and devein prawns, discard heads, reserve shells. Remove lobster meat from shell, reserve shell. Reserve prawn and lobster meat for soup. Combine reserved prawn and lobster shells, fish heads and bones, onion, celery, carrot, bay leaves, lemon thyme sprigs and water in pan, simmer, uncovered, 35 minutes. Strain stock, discard fish heads and bones and vegetables. You will need 1.5 litres (6 cups) stock.

4. Cut reserved lobster meat and fish into 4cm pieces. Add fish pieces to soup, simmer 1 minute, add lobster and reserved prawns, simmer further minute. Add scallops, bring to boil, stir in parsley and juice.
Serves 6.

- Soup best made just before serving. Stock can be made a day ahead.
- Storage: Covered, in refrigerator.
- Freeze: Stock suitable.
- Microwave: Suitable.

2. Divide dough into quarters. Roll each quarter until 2mm thick. Cut into 8cm rounds with decorative cutter.

3. Spoon 1½ teaspoons of filling into centre of each round, brush edges with a little water, fold rounds in half, press edges to seal. Place turnovers on lightly greased oven trays, brush with combined egg yolk and milk, bake in moderately hot oven about 20 minutes or until lightly browned; cool on trays. Turnovers can be served warm or cold.

Plate, fruit dish and wine jug from Corso de Fiori.

4. Filling: Combine all ingredients in bowl; mix well.

Makes about 28.

- ■ Recipe can be made 2 days ahead.
- ■ Storage: Covered, in refrigerator.
- ■ Freeze: Uncooked turnovers suitable.
- ■ Microwave: Not suitable.

CHEESE TURNOVERS

Tiropitakia

1½ cups (225g) self-raising flour
1½ cups (225g) plain flour
¾ cup (180ml) olive oil
¾ cup (180ml) warm water
1 egg yolk
2 teaspoons milk

FILLING
100g feta cheese, grated
½ cup (100g) ricotta cheese
1 egg, lightly beaten
pinch ground nutmeg
ground black pepper

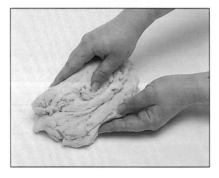

1. Sift flours into bowl, stir in oil and water, mix to soft dough. Knead dough on lightly floured surface until smooth. Cover, refrigerate 1 hour.

China, basket and serviette from Corso de Fiori.

CHICKEN SOUP WITH EGG AND LEMON

Kotosoupa me Avgolemono

The reserved chicken in this recipe can be frozen and used in the creamy chicken pie recipe (see Index).

1.4kg chicken
4 litres (16 cups) water
2 black peppercorns
1 medium carrot, chopped
1 medium onion, chopped
1 stick celery, chopped
½ cup (100g) short-grain rice
salt, pepper
2 eggs
¼ cup (60ml) lemon juice

1. Combine chicken, water, peppercorns, carrot, onion and celery in large pan, simmer, covered, 2 hours.

2. Remove chicken from pan, reserve for another use. Strain stock through sieve; discard vegetables. Cool stock, cover, refrigerate overnight. Skim fat from stock. You will need 2.25 litres (9 cups) stock.

3. Bring stock to boil in pan, add rice, cook, partly covered, about 15 minutes or until rice is tender, stirring occasionally. Add salt and pepper to taste.

4. Just before serving, whisk eggs and juice in bowl until frothy. Gradually whisk in 2 cups (500ml) of the hot stock. Whisk egg and lemon mixture into remaining hot stock and rice mixture, whisk over heat until heated through; do not boil.

Serves 6 to 8.

- Soup best made just before serving. Stock can be made 2 days ahead.
- Storage: Covered, in refrigerator.
- Freeze: Stock suitable.
- Microwave: Suitable.

Soup plate from Corso de Fiori; curtain fabric from Sandy de Beyer.

2. Heat oil in pan, add onions and garlic, cook, stirring, until soft. Add carrots and celery, cook over low heat, stirring mixture occasionally, 10 minutes. Stir in tomatoes, crumbled stock cubes and paste.

3. Add beans and hot water, simmer, covered, about 1½ hours or until beans are tender. Stir in about two-thirds of the parsley; add salt and pepper to taste. Sprinkle soup with remaining parsley.

Serves 8 to 10.

- Recipe can be made a day ahead.
- Storage: Covered, in refrigerator.
- Freeze: Suitable.
- Microwave: Suitable.

HARICOT BEAN SOUP

Fassoulatha

2 cups (400g) dried haricot beans
1 tablespoon olive oil
2 medium onions, finely chopped
1 clove garlic, crushed
2 large carrots, finely chopped
2 sticks celery, finely chopped
1.5kg tomatoes, peeled, seeded, chopped
2 vegetable stock cubes
⅓ cup (80ml) tomato paste
2.5 litres (10 cups) hot water
¼ cup chopped fresh flat-leafed parsley
salt, pepper

1. Place beans in bowl, cover well with water, cover, stand overnight. Drain beans, rinse well.

CHEESE AND OLIVE LOAF

Tiropita me Elies

1 cup (150g) self-raising flour
⅔ cup (50g) grated parmesan cheese
2 tablespoons chopped fresh mint
½ teaspoon ground black pepper
1 cup (160g) pitted black
   olives, chopped
75g mortadella, chopped
4 eggs, lightly beaten
80g butter, melted

1. Lightly grease 8cm x 26cm bar cake pan. Sift flour into bowl, add cheese, mint, pepper, olives and mortadella.

2. Stir in eggs and butter, mix until well combined. Spread mixture into prepared pan, bake, uncovered, in moderately hot oven about 35 minutes or until lightly browned and cooked through. Turn onto wire rack to cool.

Makes 1 loaf.

■ Recipe can be made a day ahead.
■ Storage: Covered, in refrigerator.
■ Freeze: Suitable.
■ Microwave: Not suitable.

Bowl from Corso de Fiori; place mats from The Caspian Studio.

PRANWS WITH FETA

excellent!

Garithes me Feta

24 (about 1.4kg) large
   uncooked prawns
2 tablespoons olive oil
4 green shallots, chopped
2 teaspoons grated lemon rind
1 teaspoon lemon pepper
1 tablespoon chopped fresh oregano
1 tablespoon chopped fresh parsley
1 tablespoon chopped fresh thyme
2 medium tomatoes, peeled,
   seeded, chopped
200g feta cheese, crumbled

TOMATO SAUCE
30g butter
1 medium onion, finely chopped
4 cloves garlic, crushed
425g can tomatoes
2 tablespoons tomato paste
⅓ cup (80ml) dry white wine
½ cup (125ml) chicken stock
½ teaspoon sugar

1. Shell prawns, leaving tails intact. Remove dark vein using knife.

2. Heat oil in large pan, add prawns, shallots, rind and pepper, cook, stirring, until prawns change colour.

3. Stir in the tomato sauce, herbs and tomatoes, stir over heat until heated through. Serve sprinkled with cheese.

4. Tomato Sauce: Heat butter in pan, add onion and garlic, cook, stirring, until onion is soft. Add undrained crushed tomatoes and remaining ingredients; stir until boiling. Blend or process sauce until smooth; strain.

Serves 6.

- Tomato sauce can be made a day ahead.
- Storage: Covered, in refrigerator.
- Freeze: Not suitable.
- Microwave: Tomato sauce suitable.

2. Shallow-fry level ¼ cups (60ml) of mixture in hot oil until lightly browned underneath; flatten slightly. Turn fritters, cook until well browned on other side and cooked through; drain on absorbent paper. Serve fritters with yogurt dip.

3. Yogurt Dip: Combine all ingredients in bowl; mix well.

Makes about 15.

■ Recipe best made close to serving.
■ Freeze: Not suitable.
■ Microwave: Not suitable.

ZUCCHINI FRITTERS WITH YOGURT DIP

*Kolokithokeftethes
me Tzatziki*

5 large (about 750g) zucchini, grated
1 medium onion, grated
½ cup (75g) plain flour
3 eggs, lightly beaten
1 tablespoon chopped fresh oregano
1 tablespoon chopped fresh basil
1 tablespoon chopped fresh parsley
salt, pepper
oil for shallow-frying

YOGURT DIP
¾ cup (180ml) plain yogurt
1 small green cucumber,
    seeded, grated
1 clove garlic, crushed
1 tablespoon chopped fresh mint
2 teaspoons lemon juice

1. Combine zucchini, onion, flour, eggs, herbs and salt and pepper to taste in bowl.

Plate from Accoutrement.

VINE LEAVES WITH PINE NUTS AND CURRANTS

Dolmathakia Lathera

Vine leaves are available from delicatessens and supermarkets.

300g packet vine leaves in brine
1 tablespoon lemon juice
¾ cup (180ml) water
1 tablespoon olive oil

FILLING
¼ cup (60ml) olive oil
1 medium onion, finely chopped
2 tablespoons pine nuts
½ cup (100g) short-grain rice
2 tablespoons currants
½ cup (125ml) water
2 tablespoons chopped fresh parsley

1. Rinse vine leaves under cold water; drain well. Place vine leaves vein side up on bench, place 2 level teaspoons of filling on each leaf, roll up firmly, folding in sides, to enclose filling.

2. Place rolls in single layer over base of heavy-based pan, add combined juice, water and oil. Place a plate on top of rolls to keep rolls in position during cooking. Simmer, covered, over low heat 1 hour.

3. Filling: Heat oil in pan, add onion, cook, stirring, until soft. Add nuts, cook, stirring, until lightly browned. Stir in rice and currants, mix well to coat rice in oil. Add water, simmer, covered, over low heat about 10 minutes or until liquid is absorbed, remove pan from heat; cool mixture. Stir in parsley.

Makes about 24.

■ Recipe can be made 4 days ahead.
■ Storage: Covered, in refrigerator.
■ Freeze: Not suitable.
■ Microwave: Not suitable.

Lemon decoration from Accoutrement.

MUSSELS WITH FENNEL AND RICE

Mithia me Maratho ke Rizi

24 (about 650g) small mussels
½ cup (125ml) dry white wine
2 tablespoons olive oil
1 small onion, chopped
2 cloves garlic, crushed
¾ cup (150g) short-grain rice
2 teaspoons grated lemon rind
½ cup (125ml) dry white wine, extra
¼ cup (60ml) water
½ small fennel bulb, finely chopped
1 tablespoon chopped fresh parsley
1½ tablespoons chopped fresh mint
pinch ground allspice
salt, pepper

3. Heat oil in pan, add onion and garlic, cook, stirring, until onion is soft. Add rice and rind, cook, stirring, until rice is coated with oil. Add combined reserved mussel liquid, extra wine and water. Bring to boil, cover with tight-fitting lid, cook over very low heat about 18 minutes or until liquid is absorbed and rice is just tender. Stand, covered, 5 minutes.

1. Scrub mussels, remove beards.

4. Transfer rice to bowl; cool. Stir in fennel, herbs and allspice, add salt and pepper to taste; mix well.

2. Add wine to large pan, bring to boil, add mussels, cook, covered, over medium heat about 2 minutes or until mussels open; drain, reserve ¾ cup (180ml) liquid.

5. Remove mussels from shells, discard half of each shell. Fill remaining shells evenly with rice mixture, top with mussels. Serves 4 to 6.

- Recipe best made close to serving.
- Freeze: Not suitable.
- Microwave: Not suitable.

EGGPLANT DIP

Melitzanosalata

1 large eggplant
1 medium onion, finely chopped
¾ cup (75g) packaged breadcrumbs
2 tablespoons plain yogurt
3 cloves garlic, crushed
½ cup chopped fresh parsley
1 tablespoon cider vinegar
1½ tablespoons lemon juice
½ cup (125ml) olive oil

1. Place whole eggplant on oven tray, bake in hot oven about 1 hour or until soft. Remove eggplant from oven; cool slightly. Peel eggplant, chop flesh roughly.

2. Combine eggplant flesh with remaining ingredients in food processor, process until smooth. Refrigerate mixture several hours or overnight.

Makes about 1½ cups.

■ Recipe can be made 2 days ahead.
■ Storage: Covered, in refrigerator.
■ Freeze: Not suitable.
■ Microwave: Not suitable.

MUSHROOM FILLO TRIANGLES

Bourekakia me Manitaria

60g butter
1 large onion, chopped
750g flat mushrooms, chopped
¼ cup (20g) grated parmesan cheese
⅓ cup (25g) stale breadcrumbs
salt, pepper
14 sheets fillo pastry
100g butter, melted, extra

1. Heat butter in pan, add onion, cook, stirring, until soft. Add mushrooms, cook, stirring, until mushrooms are tender and liquid evaporated. Remove from heat, stir in cheese, breadcrumbs and salt and pepper to taste; mix well.

2. To prevent pastry from drying out, cover with a damp tea-towel until you are ready to use it. Layer 2 sheets of pastry together, brushing each with a little extra butter. Cut layered sheets into 4 strips lengthways. Place 1 tablespoon of mushroom mixture at 1 end of each strip.

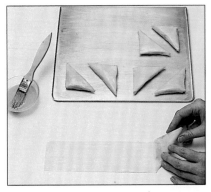

3. Fold 1 corner end of pastry diagonally across filling to other edge to form a triangle. Continue folding to end of strip, retaining triangular shape. Brush triangles with a little more extra butter. Repeat with remaining pastry, filling and extra butter. Place triangles on greased oven trays. Bake in moderately hot oven about 15 minutes or until browned.

Makes 28.

- Recipe can be made a day ahead.
- Storage: Covered, in refrigerator.
- Freeze: Uncooked triangles suitable.
- Microwave: Not suitable.

Plate from Montague North; rug from Zante Imports.

PICKLED OLIVES

Elies se Armi

Pickled olives are ready to eat after approximately 5 weeks in salted water. Do not mix black (ripe) and green olives when pickling them.

1.5kg fresh black or green olives
⅓ cup (75g) fine sea salt
1 litre (4 cups) water
½ cup (125ml) olive oil

1. Discard over-blemished olives. Make 2 cuts lengthways into each olive, through to stone, using sharp knife.

2. Add olives to sterilised jars (2 litre/8 cup capacity) until jars are two-thirds full. Cover olives with water. Fill a small plastic bag with water, tie bag securely, sit bag on top of olives to keep olives submerged.

3. Scum will appear on surface of water.

4. Change water in jars every day. Refill jars with water. Continue changing water for 4 days for black olives and for 6 days for green olives.

5. Combine salt and the 1 litre (4 cups) of water in pan, stir until salt dissolves; cool.

6. Drain water from jars, pour in enough salted water to cover olives.

7. Pour enough oil into jars to cover olives and seal completely.

- Pickled olives should be made at least 5 weeks ahead.
- Storage: Covered, in a cool, dark place for up to 6 months.
- Freeze: Not suitable.

MARINATED OLIVES

Elies me Skordo

It is necessary to pickle olives before marinating them. Marinated olives (pictured at left) are ready to eat after approximately 2 weeks in oil mixture.

600g drained black or green pickled olives
1 clove garlic, sliced
2 lemon wedges
1 sprig fresh dill
2 cups (500ml) olive oil

1. Combine olives, garlic, lemon and dill in jar (1 litre/4 cup capacity); add oil, seal jar.

- Marinated olives should be made approximately 2 weeks ahead.
- Storage: Covered, in cool, dark place for up to 2 months.
- Freeze: Not suitable.

EASTER SOUP

Mayeritsa

After the Lenten fast, this soup is traditionally eaten at the celebration that follows the midnight Resurrection Service.

1 tablespoon olive oil
1kg lamb shanks
3 litres (12 cups) cold water
1 medium onion, quartered
1 teaspoon black peppercorns
2 bay leaves
150g lambs' heart
150g lambs' fry
150g honeycomb tripe
60g butter
6 green shallots, chopped
1 clove garlic, crushed
⅓ cup (65g) short-grain rice
2 tablespoons chopped fresh dill
2 tablespoons chopped fresh parsley
salt, pepper
3 eggs
⅔ cup (160ml) lemon juice
¼ cup (60ml) water, extra

1. Heat oil in pan, add shanks, cook until well browned all over. Remove pan from heat, add water, onion, black peppercorns and bay leaves. Return pan to heat, simmer gently, uncovered, 1½ hours. Strain and reserve stock. You will need 1.75 litres (7 cups) stock. Remove meat from shanks, chop meat into small pieces. Discard bones and onion mixture.

2. Chop heart, fry and tripe into very small pieces. Add tripe to pan of boiling water, boil, uncovered, 1 minute; remove tripe from pan with slotted spoon. Add heart and fry to same pan, boil 1 minute; drain.

3. Heat butter in pan, add shallots, garlic, tripe, heart and fry, cook, stirring, until shallots are soft; remove from pan. Add reserved stock to same pan, bring to boil add rice, simmer, uncovered, until rice is tender. Stir in shallot mixture, lamb and herbs; add salt and pepper to taste.

4. Lightly whisk eggs in bowl, gradually whisk in combined juice and extra water. Whisk about 1 cup (250ml) hot soup into egg mixture, whisk egg mixture into soup in pan; do not boil.

Serves 6 to 8.

- Recipe can be made, without egg mixture, a day ahead.
- Storage: Covered, in refrigerator.
- Freeze: Stock suitable.
- Microwave: Not suitable.

TOMATO SOUP WITH VERMICELLI

Soupa me Fithe

3 litres (12 cups) water
4 lamb shanks
1 medium onion, chopped
4 black peppercorns
2 bay leaves
4 medium tomatoes, finely chopped
¼ cup (60ml) tomato paste
¼ teaspoon sugar
salt, pepper
100g rice vermicelli noodles

1. Combine water, shanks, onion, peppercorns and bay leaves in large pan. Simmer, partly covered, 1½ hours. Strain stock into bowl, discard shank mixture. Cool stock, cover, refrigerate several hours or overnight. Skim fat from stock. You will need 1.75 litres (7 cups) stock.

2. Bring stock to boil in pan, stir in tomatoes, paste, sugar and salt and pepper to taste. Simmer, partly covered, 40 minutes.

3. Strain soup, push tomato mixture through sieve; discard seeds and pulp.

4. Return soup to pan, bring to boil, add noodles, simmer, stirring occasionally, until noodles are tender.

Serves 6 to 8.

■ Stock best made a day ahead.
■ Storage: Covered, in refrigerator.
■ Freeze: Stock suitable.
■ Microwave: Suitable.

SALADS & VEGETABLES

SALATES KE LAHANIKA

Fresh, home-grown vegetables are much prized, and provide the inspiration for well-flavoured, satisfying recipes. Some dishes are hearty main meals; others can be served as accompaniments. Of the salads, possibly the best known is the classic Greek salad with feta cheese, tomatoes, onion, cucumbers and olives, etc., but there are many other tempting salads to enjoy. This section also includes tasty recipes using rice and pasta.

RICE WITH LEEK AND SILVERBEET

Spanakorizo

¼ cup (60ml) olive oil
1 large leek, sliced
2 cloves garlic, crushed
1½ cups (300g) short-grain rice
3 cups (750ml) water
1 bunch silverbeet
2 tablespoons lemon juice
¼ cup chopped fresh parsley
salt, pepper

2. Remove silverbeet leaves from stalks, discard stalks. Slice leaves thinly; wash well. Place silverbeet in separate pan, simmer, covered, few minutes or until just limp; drain.

3. Stir silverbeet, juice and parsley into rice; add salt and pepper to taste.
Serves 4 to 6.

■ Recipe best made just before serving.
■ Freeze: Not suitable.
■ Microwave: Suitable.

1. Heat oil in pan, add leek and garlic, cook, stirring, until leek is soft. Add rice, stir until rice is coated in oil. Add water, simmer, covered with tight-fitting lid, over low heat 15 minutes. Remove pan from heat, stand, covered, 5 minutes.

BROAD BEANS WITH PEAS AND ARTICHOKES

Anginares me Koukia

You need 1kg fresh peas for this recipe.

3½ cups (500g) frozen broad
    beans, thawed
2 tablespoons olive oil
1 large onion, finely chopped
4 cloves garlic, crushed
2 medium carrots, chopped
2¼ cups (350g) shelled peas
425g can tomatoes
20 drained artichoke hearts, quartered
2 tablespoons chopped fresh dill
salt, pepper

1. Add broad beans to pan of boiling water, boil 1 minute; drain, rinse under cold water until cold, drain well. Peel and discard outer skins.

2. Heat oil in pan, add onion, garlic and carrots, cook, stirring, until onion is soft. Stir in peas and undrained crushed tomatoes. Simmer, covered, about 10 minutes or until peas are tender.

3. Add beans, artichokes and dill, stir over heat until heated through. Add salt and pepper to taste.

Serves 4 to 6.

■ Recipe best made on day of serving.
■ Storage: Covered, in refrigerator.
■ Freeze: Not suitable.
■ Microwave: Suitable.

Plates from Corso de Fiori; tiles from Country Floors.

Tiles from Country Floors.

ROASTED VEGETABLES

Briami

6 medium tomatoes, peeled
3 medium potatoes
3 medium red Spanish onions
4 medium zucchini
2 sticks celery
⅓ cup chopped fresh parsley
1½ tablespoons chopped fresh dill
1 teaspoon chopped fresh mint
2 cloves garlic, crushed
salt, pepper
¼ cup (60ml) olive oil

1. Cut tomatoes into thin slices. Cut potatoes and onions into wedges. Cut zucchini in half lengthways, then into 3cm lengths. Cut celery into 3cm lengths.

2. Lightly grease a baking dish, add half the tomatoes, top with potatoes, onions, zucchini and celery. Place remaining tomatoes over vegetables.

3. Sprinkle with herbs, garlic and salt and pepper to taste; drizzle with oil. Bake, uncovered, in hot oven 30 minutes, stir gently, bake further 40 minutes or until vegetables are tender.

Serves 6.

■ Recipe can be made a day ahead.
■ Storage: Covered, in refrigerator.
■ Freeze: Not suitable.
■ Microwave: Not suitable.

COLD LENTIL SALAD

Salata Faki

2 cloves
1 medium onion
1 cup (200g) brown lentils
1 bay leaf
1 teaspoon salt
1¼ litres (5 cups) water
½ cup (125ml) olive oil
⅓ cup (80ml) white wine vinegar
2 teaspoons dried oregano leaves
2 green shallots, chopped
2 sticks celery, finely chopped
6 lettuce leaves

Serves 4 to 6.

- Recipe can be made a day ahead.
- Storage: Covered, in refrigerator.
- Freeze: Not suitable.
- Microwave: Lentils suitable.

1. Press cloves into onion. Combine onion, lentils, bay leaf, salt and water in pan. Simmer, uncovered, about 20 minutes or until lentils are just tender; drain, discard onion and bay leaf.

2. Transfer hot lentils to bowl, stir in combined oil, vinegar and oregano. Cool, cover, refrigerate until cold.

3. Stir in shallots and celery; mix well. Place lettuce in bowl, top with lentil salad.

BRAISED VEGETABLES

Yachni

¼ cup (60ml) olive oil
2 large onions, chopped
1 clove garlic, crushed
5 medium tomatoes, chopped
3 medium potatoes, quartered
¾ cup (180ml) tomato puree
1 cup (250ml) water
250g okra
300g green beans
½ medium cauliflower, chopped
2 tablespoons chopped fresh
    flat-leafed parsley
½ teaspoon sugar
salt, pepper

1. Heat oil in pan, add onions and garlic, cook, covered, over low heat, stirring occasionally, until onions are very soft.

2. Add tomatoes to pan, simmer, covered, about 10 minutes or until soft. Add potatoes, puree, water, okra and beans, simmer, covered, 15 minutes.

3. Add cauliflower, simmer, covered, until potatoes and cauliflower are tender. Stir in parsley, sugar and salt and pepper to taste, stir until hot.

Serves 6.

■ Recipe can be made a day ahead.
■ Storage: Covered, in refrigerator.
■ Freeze: Not suitable.
■ Microwave: Suitable.

Dish from Country Floors.

China from Corso de Fiori.

BEETROOT SALAD WITH GARLIC SAUCE

Bantzaria Salata me Skorthalia

8 medium (about 1.6kg) fresh
    beetroot with leaves
2 tablespoons olive oil
1 tablespoon lemon juice
salt, pepper

GARLIC SAUCE
2 medium potatoes
6 cloves garlic, crushed
2 slices white bread
⅓ cup (80ml) olive oil
1 tablespoon lemon juice
1 tablespoon white wine vinegar
salt, pepper

3. Garlic Sauce: Boil, steam or microwave potatoes until tender; drain, mash potatoes in bowl. Press potato through a fine sieve to remove any lumps. Combine potato and garlic in bowl; mix well.

1. Wash beetroot well, cut off leaves, reserve leaves. Add unpeeled beetroot to large pan of boiling water, boil, uncovered, about 15 minutes or until tender; drain, rinse under cold water, drain well. Peel beetroot while warm; cut into wedges.

4. Trim crusts from bread. Soak bread in cold water 2 minutes; drain, squeeze water from bread. Add bread to potato mixture, beat until smooth. Gradually add combined oil, juice and vinegar with salt and pepper to taste; beat until smooth.

Serves 4 to 6.

■ Recipe can be prepared a day ahead.
■ Storage: Covered, in refrigerator.
■ Freeze: Not suitable.
■ Microwave: Beetroot and
    potatoes suitable.

2. Heat oil in pan add reserved beetroot leaves, cook, stirring, few minutes or until leaves are just wilted. Add juice, beetroot and salt and pepper to taste; stir until combined. Transfer mixture to bowl, serve warm or cold with garlic sauce.

Plates and rug from Zante Imports.

CAULIFLOWER WITH FRESH HERB VINAIGRETTE

Kounoupithi me Aromatica

1 medium cauliflower
¾ cup (180ml) olive oil
¼ cup (60ml) white wine vinegar
1 tablespoon lemon juice
2 tablespoons chopped fresh dill
1 tablespoon chopped fresh parsley
salt, pepper

1. Cut cauliflower into small flowerets. Boil, steam or microwave cauliflower until just tender; rinse under cold water, drain.

2. Combine oil, vinegar, juice and herbs in bowl, add salt and pepper to taste; mix well. Pour dressing over cauliflower in bowl; mix well, cover, refrigerate until cold.

Serves 4 to 6.

■ Recipe can be prepared a day ahead.
■ Storage: Covered, in refrigerator.
■ Freeze: Not suitable.
■ Microwave: Cauliflower suitable.

GREEK SALAD

Horiatiki Salata

250g feta cheese
5 medium tomatoes
1 large red Spanish onion, sliced
2 small green cucumbers,
   thickly sliced
1 cup (160g) black olives

DRESSING
½ cup (125ml) olive oil
¼ cup (60ml) white vinegar
1 clove garlic, crushed
1 teaspoon sugar
1 teaspoon chopped fresh oregano

1. Cut cheese into small cubes, cut tomatoes into wedges. Combine cheese, tomatoes, onion, cucumbers and olives in bowl; drizzle with dressing.

2. Dressing: Combine all ingredients in bowl; mix well.

Serves 6.

■ Recipe best made just before serving.
■ Freeze: Not suitable.

Tiles and platter from Country Floors.

BAKED TOMATOES WITH NUTTY RICE FILLING

Yemistes Domates

10 medium tomatoes
2 tablespoons olive oil
1 large onion, finely chopped
¼ cup (35g) currants
¼ cup (40g) pine nuts
¾ cup (150g) short-grain rice
1 cup (250ml) water
1 tablespoon chopped fresh dill
1 tablespoon chopped fresh thyme
1 tablespoon chopped fresh parsley
salt, pepper

WHITE SAUCE
30g butter
2½ tablespoons plain flour
1⅓ cups (330ml) milk
salt, pepper

1. Cut tops from tomatoes; tops are not used in this recipe. Spoon pulp, seeds and juice into bowl; mash. Reserve 1½ cups (375ml) of pulp mixture.

2. Heat oil in pan, add onion, cook, stirring, until onion is soft. Add currants, nuts, rice and water, simmer, covered with tight-fitting lid, 8 minutes. Remove pan from heat, stir in herbs and reserved pulp mixture; add salt and pepper to taste.

3. Divide rice mixture between tomatoes, top with white sauce. Place tomatoes in ovenproof dish with enough boiling water to come 1cm up the sides of the tomatoes. Bake, uncovered, in moderately slow oven about 40 minutes or until tomatoes are lightly browned and heated through.

4. White Sauce: Melt butter in pan, add flour, stir over heat until mixture is dry and grainy. Remove pan from heat, gradually stir in milk, add salt and pepper to taste; stir over heat until mixture boils and thickens; cool slightly.

Makes 10.

■ Recipe best made just before serving.
■ Freeze: Not suitable.
■ Microwave: Not suitable.

SPAGHETTI WITH BURNT BUTTER SAUCE

Makaronia me Voutiro

500g spaghetti pasta
125g butter
2 cloves garlic, crushed
salt, pepper
½ cup (50g) grated hard
 goats' cheese
2 tablespoons grated hard
 goats' cheese, extra

1. Add pasta to large pan of boiling water, boil, uncovered, until just tender; drain.

2. Heat butter in pan, cook, stirring, until butter is lightly browned; remove pan from heat, stir in garlic and salt and pepper to taste. Toss hot pasta with butter mixture and cheese. Sprinkle with extra cheese.

Serves 4.

■ Recipe best made just before serving.
■ Freeze: Not suitable.
■ Microwave: Spaghetti suitable.

SPRING SALAD

Prasini Salata

8 green shallots, finely chopped
1 tablespoon finely chopped
    fennel bulb
1 tablespoon chopped fresh parsley
1 tablespoon chopped fresh dill
1 medium cos lettuce
½ cup (125ml) olive oil
¼ cup (60ml) white vinegar
1 clove garlic, crushed
salt, pepper

1. Combine shallots, fennel, parsley, dill and finely shredded lettuce in bowl.

2. Add combined oil, vinegar and garlic with salt and pepper to taste; mix well.

Serves 4.

◼ Recipe best made just before serving.
◼ Freeze: Not suitable.

SPAGHETTI WITH CHICK PEAS AND SPINACH

Makaronia me Revithia ke Spanaki

1 cup (200g) dried chick peas
250g spaghetti pasta
1 cup (250ml) olive oil
1 medium red Spanish onion, sliced
3 cloves garlic, crushed
1 bunch (about 650g) English
    spinach, finely shredded
3 teaspoons grated lemon rind
2 tablespoons lemon juice
3 medium tomatoes, peeled,
    seeded, sliced
2 tablespoons chopped fresh parsley
2 tablespoons chopped fresh mint
salt, pepper

1. Place peas in bowl, cover well with water, cover, stand overnight. Drain peas, place in pan, cover well with water, simmer, uncovered, about 20 minutes or until tender. Drain peas, rinse under cold water; drain. Add pasta to large pan of boiling water, boil, uncovered, until tender; drain, rinse under cold water, drain.

2. Heat ¼ cup (60ml) of the oil in pan, add onion and garlic, cook, stirring, until onion is soft. Add spinach, stir over heat few minutes or until just wilted.

3. Stir in remaining oil, rind, juice, tomatoes, peas and pasta; stir until hot. Stir in herbs and salt and pepper to taste.

Serves 4 to 6.

- Chick peas best prepared a day ahead.
- Storage: Covered, at room temperature.
- Freeze: Not suitable.
- Microwave: Spaghetti suitable.

Plates and jug from Zante Imports; copper plate from Parker's of Turramurra.

MAIN COURSES

FAYITA

Garlic, lemons, olive oil, spices and herbs add lots of wonderful Greek flavour to robust dishes using chicken, seafood, lamb, beef, pork, veal and more. They are fresh, colourful and simple to prepare, giving you a tantalising taste experience of many favourite recipes. With generous servings, these dishes are great family fare, yet would be very popular for dinner parties, too.

ROAST CHICKEN WITH LEMON PISTACHIO RICE

Kotopoulo Yemisto

1.4kg chicken
4 large potatoes
¼ cup (60ml) olive oil
2 teaspoons chopped fresh thyme
freshly ground black pepper

SEASONING
¼ cup (60ml) olive oil
1 medium onion, chopped
⅓ cup (65g) long-grain rice
1 cup (250ml) chicken stock
1 cup (150g) pistachios
2 teaspoons chopped fresh thyme
2 teaspoons grated lemon rind

2. Cut potatoes into 1cm slices. Place potato slices around chicken in dish. Drizzle chicken and potatoes with oil; sprinkle potatoes with thyme and pepper. Bake in moderate oven further 1 hour or until chicken is tender. Remove chicken from dish; keep warm.

4. Seasoning: Heat oil in pan, add onion, cook, stirring, until soft. Stir in rice until coated with oil. Stir in stock, simmer, covered, about 20 minutes or until rice is tender and liquid absorbed. Remove from heat, stir in nuts, thyme and rind; cool.

Serves 4.

■ Seasoning can be made a day ahead.
■ Storage: Covered, in refrigerator.
■ Freeze: Seasoning suitable.
■ Microwave: Not suitable.

1. Place seasoning in chicken, tie legs together, tuck wings under body. Place chicken, breast side up, in large baking dish, bake in moderate oven 40 minutes.

3. Bake potatoes in very hot oven further 15 minutes or until potatoes are browned and crisp. Serve roast chicken with potatoes.

CHICKEN WITH SPINACH AND FETA

*Kotopoulo me Spanaki
ke Feta*

¾ bunch (about 500g)
  English spinach
75g feta cheese, crumbled
4 single chicken breast fillets
1 tablespoon olive oil
⅓ cup (80ml) cream
2 tablespoons chopped fresh parsley

SAUCE
60g butter
2 tablespoons plain flour
1 cup (250ml) chicken stock
1 cup (250ml) dry white wine

3. Heat oil in pan, add chicken, cook until browned. Stir in sauce, simmer, covered, 25 minutes. Stir in cream and parsley, stir until heated through.

1. Add washed spinach to pan, cook, stirring, until just wilted; drain well, cool.

4. Sauce: Melt butter in pan, add flour, stir over heat until bubbling. Remove from heat, gradually stir in stock and wine, stir over heat until sauce boils and thickens.

Serves 4.

■ Chicken can be prepared several hours ahead.
■ Storage: Covered, in refrigerator.
■ Freeze: Not suitable.
■ Microwave: Spinach and sauce suitable.

2. Combine spinach and cheese in bowl. Cut pocket in side of chicken, fill with spinach mixture; secure with toothpicks.

CREAMY CHICKEN PIE

Kotopita

60g butter
4 bacon rashers, chopped
6 green shallots, chopped
2 cloves garlic, crushed
2 tablespoons plain flour
1½ cups (375ml) milk
3½ cups (525g) chopped cooked chicken
⅓ cup (25g) grated parmesan cheese
2 eggs, lightly beaten
10 sheets fillo pastry
80g butter, melted, extra

1. Lightly grease 23cm pie dish. Heat butter in pan, add bacon, shallots and garlic, cook, stirring, until bacon is crisp. Add flour, stir until combined. Remove from heat, gradually stir in milk, stir over heat until mixture boils and thickens; cool. Stir in chicken, cheese and eggs.

2. To prevent pastry from drying out, cover with a damp tea-towel until ready to use. Layer 2 sheets of pastry together, brushing each with a little extra butter. Fold layered sheets in half lengthways, place in prepared dish with edges overhanging. Repeat with another 6 pastry sheets and more extra butter, overlapping strips clockwise around dish until covered.

3. Spoon chicken mixture into dish, fold overhanging edges back onto filling; brush all over with more extra butter.

4. Layer remaining 2 pastry sheets with more extra butter, fold in half crossways, buttered sides together. Place pastry on top of pie, trim edge. Brush top lightly with more extra butter, bake in moderate oven about 35 minutes or until browned and heated through; cover with foil if pie begins to over-brown.

Serves 6 to 8.

- Recipe can be prepared a day ahead.
- Storage: Covered, in refrigerator.
- Freeze: Not suitable.
- Microwave: Not suitable.

Copper plate and bowl from Parker's of Turramurra; rug from Zante Imports.

CHICKEN WITH FIGS IN RED WINE

Kotopoulo Krasato me Sika

8 chicken thigh cutlets
2 tablespoons plain flour
1½ teaspoons ground coriander
pinch cayenne pepper
1½ teaspoons ground cumin
⅓ cup (80ml) olive oil
2 medium onions, sliced
6 cloves garlic
2 bay leaves
8 fresh figs
1¼ cups (310ml) dry red wine
1 teaspoon chicken stock powder
2 teaspoons grated lemon rind
1 teaspoon lemon juice
2 teaspoons cornflour
1 tablespoon water
2 tablespoons chopped fresh
   flat-leafed parsley

1. Remove skin from chicken. Toss chicken in combined flour and spices, shake away excess flour. Heat oil in pan, add chicken in batches, cook until well browned all over; drain on absorbent paper. Add onions and garlic to same pan, cook, covered, over low heat, stirring occasionally, about 10 minutes or until onions are very soft.

2. Transfer chicken and onion mixture to large heatproof dish (1.75 litre/7 cup capacity). Add bay leaves, figs and combined wine and stock powder, cook, covered, in moderate oven about 1¼ hours or until chicken is very tender.

3. Remove chicken, figs and bay leaves from dish; discard bay leaves. Add rind, juice and blended cornflour and water, stir over heat until mixture boils and thickens.

4. Return chicken and figs to pan stir until heated through; sprinkle with parsley.

Serves 4.

- Recipe can be made a day ahead.
- Storage: Covered, in refrigerator.
- Freeze: Suitable.
- Microwave: Not suitable.

ROAST QUAIL IN VINE LEAVES

Ortikia se Klimatofila

Vine leaves are available from delicatessens and supermarkets.

12 quail
2 tablespoons grated lemon rind
1 tablespoon grated orange rind
½ cup (125ml) honey
⅓ cup (80ml) olive oil
½ cup (125ml) lemon juice
⅓ cup (80ml) orange juice
¼ cup chopped fresh lemon thyme
½ cup (125ml) brandy
salt, pepper
24 packaged vine leaves in brine

3. Place quail in baking dish, bake, uncovered, in moderately hot oven about 35 minutes or until tender, basting with reserved marinade every 10 minutes. Serve quail drizzled with pan juices.

Serves 6.

- Quail best marinated a day ahead.
- Storage: Covered, in refrigerator.
- Freeze: Uncooked marinated quail suitable.
- Microwave: Not suitable.

1. Place quail in large bowl, pour over combined rinds, honey, oil, juices, thyme, brandy and salt and pepper to taste. Cover, refrigerate 3 hours or overnight.

2. Rinse vine leaves under cold water; drain, pat dry with absorbent paper. Remove quail from marinade; reserve marinade. Fold wings under quail, fold vine leaves in half crossways. Wrap 2 leaves around each quail, secure legs together with toothpicks.

Plate from Accoutrement.

Plate and rug from Zante Imports.

RABBIT WITH APRICOTS AND CRACKED WHEAT

Kouneli me Verikoko ke Pligouri

1⅓ cups (200g) dried apricots
¾ cup (180ml) dry white wine
2kg rabbit pieces
plain flour
⅓ cup (80ml) olive oil
2 large onions, sliced
2 cloves garlic, crushed
1 tablespoon plain flour, extra
2 bay leaves
3 sticks celery, chopped
2½ cups (625ml) chicken stock
2 teaspoons honey
2 teaspoons chopped fresh thyme
2 teaspoons chopped fresh rosemary
2 teaspoons coriander
    seeds, crushed
1 tablespoon brown vinegar
2 teaspoons chopped fresh
    thyme, extra
2 teaspoons chopped fresh
    rosemary, extra
salt, pepper

CRACKED WHEAT
2 tablespoons olive oil
2 cups (500ml) water
1 cup (160g) cracked wheat
½ cup (80g) black olives, sliced
2 tablespoons chopped fresh parsley
salt, pepper

1. Combine apricots and wine in bowl, cover, stand 1 hour.

2. Toss rabbit in flour, shake away excess flour. Heat oil in pan, add rabbit in batches, cook until browned all over. Transfer rabbit to ovenproof dish (3 litre/12 cup capacity); reserve pan. Add onions and garlic to reserved pan, cook, stirring, until onions are soft. Stir in extra flour, cook until grainy.

3. Gradually stir in bay leaves, celery, stock, undrained apricots, honey, thyme, rosemary, seeds and vinegar. Bring to boil, pour mixture over rabbit, stir well.

4. Bake, covered, in moderately hot oven about 2 hours or until rabbit is tender. Stir in extra thyme and extra rosemary; add salt and pepper to taste. Serve rabbit with cracked wheat.

5. Cracked Wheat: Combine oil and water in pan, bring to boil, add wheat, simmer, covered, over low heat 15 minutes. Remove from heat, stand, covered, 10 minutes. Add olives, parsley and salt and pepper to taste, stir lightly with fork.

Serves 6.

■ Recipe can be made a day ahead.
■ Storage: Covered, in refrigerator.
■ Freeze: Suitable.
■ Microwave: Not suitable.

GREEK SAUSAGES IN TOMATO SAUCE

Souzoukakia

800g minced beef
1 cup (70g) stale breadcrumbs
1 medium onion, finely chopped
2 cloves garlic, crushed
2 tablespoons chopped fresh thyme
2 tablespoons chopped fresh oregano
½ teaspoon ground cumin
1 egg, lightly beaten
salt, pepper
2 tablespoons olive oil
2 tablespoons chopped fresh mint

TOMATO SAUCE
2 tablespoons olive oil
1 medium onion, finely chopped
2 cloves garlic, crushed
½ cup (125ml) dry red wine
2 x 425g cans tomatoes
⅓ cup (80ml) tomato paste
1 cup (250ml) chicken stock
2 tablespoons chopped fresh oregano
2 teaspoons sugar
pinch ground cinnamon
salt, pepper

1. Combine mince, breadcrumbs, onion, garlic, thyme, oregano, cumin and egg in bowl, add salt and pepper to taste; mix well. Roll 2 level tablespoons of mixture into sausage shape, repeat with remaining mince mixture.

2. Heat oil in pan, add sausages in batches, cook, turning, until well browned; drain on absorbent paper.

3. Place sausages in pan with tomato sauce, simmer, covered, about 10 minutes or until cooked through. Sprinkle with mint before serving.

4. Tomato Sauce: Heat oil in pan, add onion and garlic, cook, stirring, until onion is soft. Add wine, simmer, uncovered, until reduced by half. Stir in undrained crushed tomatoes and remaining ingredients with salt and pepper to taste, simmer, uncovered, about 10 minutes or until sauce is slightly thickened.

Serves 4 to 6.

■ Recipe can be made a day ahead.
■ Storage: Covered, in refrigerator.
■ Freeze: Suitable.
■ Microwave: Not suitable.

China and bowls from Accoutrement.

Plate and urn from Themelio-Salapatis.

BEEF WITH FENNEL

Kreas me Maratho

⅓ cup (80ml) olive oil
1 large onion, sliced
3 cloves garlic, sliced
1.25kg piece beef silverside
salt, pepper
½ cup (125ml) dry red wine
2 cups (500ml) beef stock
6 sprigs fresh thyme
2 bay leaves
3 sprigs fresh oregano
1½ small fennel bulbs
2 tablespoons pine nuts, toasted
¼ cup chopped fresh parsley

1. Heat half the oil in pan, add onion and garlic, cook, stirring, until onion is soft; drain on absorbent paper. Sprinkle beef with salt and pepper to taste. Heat remaining oil in same pan, add beef, cook, turning, until browned all over.

2. Return onion mixture to pan, add combined wine and stock and herbs, cook, covered, over low heat 1½ hours, turning beef once during cooking.

3. Cut fennel into wedges, place in pan with beef, cook, covered, over low heat further 30 minutes or until beef and fennel are tender. Remove beef from pan, stand 10 minutes before serving. Serve sliced beef with fennel and strained cooking liquid. Sprinkle with pine nuts and parsley. Serves 6.

■ Recipe can be prepared a day ahead.
■ Storage: Covered, in refrigerator.
■ Freeze: Not suitable.
■ Microwave: Not suitable.

PASTITSO

Pastitso

250g macaroni pasta
2 eggs, lightly beaten
¾ cup (60g) grated parmesan cheese
2 tablespoons stale breadcrumbs

MEAT SAUCE
2 tablespoons olive oil
2 medium onions, chopped
750g minced beef
425g can tomatoes
⅓ cup (80ml) tomato paste
½ cup (125ml) water
¼ cup (60ml) dry white wine
1 teaspoon beef stock powder
½ teaspoon ground cinnamon
1 egg, lightly beaten

TOPPING
90g butter
½ cup (75g) plain flour
3½ cups (875ml) milk
1 cup (80g) grated parmesan cheese
2 egg yolks

3. Meat Sauce: Heat oil in pan, add onions and mince, cook, stirring, until mince is well browned. Stir in undrained crushed tomatoes, paste, water, wine, stock powder and cinnamon, simmer, uncovered, until thick; cool. Stir in egg.

4. Topping: Melt butter in pan, add flour, stir over heat until bubbling, remove from heat, gradually stir in milk. Stir over heat until sauce boils and thickens, stir in cheese; cool slightly. Stir in egg yolks.

Serves 6 to 8.

- Pastitso can be made a day ahead.
- Storage: Covered, in refrigerator.
- Freeze: Suitable.
- Microwave: Pasta suitable.

1. Grease shallow ovenproof dish (2.5 litre/10 cup capacity). Add pasta to large pan of boiling water, boil, uncovered, until just tender; drain. Combine hot pasta, eggs and cheese in bowl; mix well. Press pasta over base of prepared dish.

2. Top pasta evenly with meat sauce, pour over topping, smooth surface; sprinkle with breadcrumbs. Bake, uncovered, in moderate oven about 1 hour or until lightly browned. Stand 10 minutes before serving.

Spoon from Corso de Fiori.

Plate and urn from Themelio-Salapatas; tiles from Country Floors.

BEEF WITH THYME AND OREGANO BUTTER

Kreas me Thimari ke Rigani

1kg piece rump steak
1 tablespoon olive oil
freshly cracked black peppercorns
salt

THYME AND OREGANO BUTTER
100g soft butter
1 tablespoon chopped fresh thyme
1 tablespoon chopped fresh oregano
1 small clove garlic, crushed
2 teaspoons lemon juice

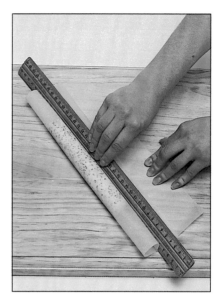

3. Fold 1 side of the paper over roll, then, with a ruler, push against the butter so that the mixture forms a smooth log. Roll the butter in the greaseproof paper, refrigerate.

Serves 6.

- Thyme and oregano butter can be made a day ahead.
- Storage: Covered, in refrigerator.
- Microwave: Not suitable.
- Freeze: Butter suitable.

1. Cut steak into 6 pieces. Brush each steak with oil, sprinkle with pepper and salt to taste. Barbecue, pan-fry or grill steaks until cooked as desired. Serve with slices of thyme and oregano butter.

2. Thyme and Oregano Butter: Beat all ingredients in small bowl with electric mixer or wooden spoon until well combined. Spoon mixture onto a sheet of greaseproof paper in a rough log shape.

ZUCCHINI AND EGGPLANT LITTLE SHOES

Papoutsakia

6 medium zucchini
6 medium lady-finger eggplants
2 tablespoons olive oil
1 medium onion, chopped
2 cloves garlic, crushed
400g minced beef
425g can tomatoes
¼ cup (60ml) tomato paste
1 cup (250ml) beef stock
⅓ cup (65g) short-grain rice
2 tablespoons chopped fresh parsley
salt, pepper
½ cup (40g) grated parmesan cheese

SAUCE
30g butter
1½ tablespoons plain flour
1 cup (250ml) milk
1 egg, lightly beaten
pinch ground nutmeg

3. Place zucchini and eggplant shells on oven trays, fill with mince mixture. Spoon sauce over mince mixture, sprinkle with cheese. Bake in moderate oven about 35 minutes or until vegetables are tender and tops are lightly browned.

1. Cut zucchini and eggplant in half lengthways, scoop out pulp with spoon, leaving thin shells; chop pulp finely.

4. Sauce: Melt butter in pan, add flour, cook, stirring, until mixture is dry and grainy. Remove from heat, gradually stir in milk, stir over heat until mixture boils and thickens. Cool, stir in egg and nutmeg.

Serves 6.

■ Recipe can be prepared a day ahead.
■ Storage: Covered, in refrigerator.
■ Freeze: Mince filling suitable.
■ Microwave: Sauce suitable.

2. Heat oil in pan, add onion and garlic, cook, stirring, until onion is soft. Add mince, cook, stirring, until well browned. Add chopped pulp, undrained crushed tomatoes, combined paste and stock. Bring to boil, stir in rice, simmer, uncovered, about 15 minutes or until rice is tender and mixture is thick; stir in parsley, salt and pepper to taste.

Plate from Accoutrement.

BRAISED BEEF AND ONIONS

Stifatho

1kg round steak
30g butter
1 tablespoon olive oil
1 medium onion, chopped
2 cloves garlic, crushed
6cm piece orange rind
410g can tomatoes
½ cup (125ml) dry red wine
2 tablespoons white vinegar
¼ teaspoon ground cinnamon
¼ teaspoon ground nutmeg
1 teaspoon sugar
½ cup (125ml) water
1 tablespoon olive oil, extra
500g baby onions

1. Cut steak into 2cm pieces. Heat half the butter and half the oil in pan, add half the steak, cook, stirring, until browned; remove from pan. Repeat with remaining butter, oil and steak; remove from pan.

2. Add chopped onion, garlic and rind to same pan, cook, stirring, until onion is soft. Stir in undrained crushed tomatoes, wine, vinegar, cinnamon, nutmeg, sugar, water and steak. Simmer, covered, 1 hour.

3. Meanwhile, heat extra oil in separate pan, add baby onions, cook, stirring, until well browned all over.

4. Add onions to steak mixture, simmer, covered, further 20 minutes or until steak and onions are tender. Remove lid, simmer further 10 minutes or until thickened slightly; remove rind before serving.

Serves 4 to 6.

■ Recipe can be made a day ahead.
■ Storage: Covered, in refrigerator.
■ Freeze: Suitable.
■ Microwave: Not suitable.

SQUID WITH RICE AND TOMATO

Kalamarakia Yemista

8 medium (about 1kg) cleaned
   squid hoods
¾ cup (180ml) tomato puree
½ cup (125ml) dry white wine
⅓ cup (25g) stale white breadcrumbs
1 tablespoon olive oil

RICE FILLING
¼ cup (60ml) olive oil
1 medium onion, finely chopped
2 cloves garlic, crushed
¾ cup (150g) short-grain rice
½ bunch (about 325g) English
   spinach, shredded
¼ teaspoon ground nutmeg
⅔ cup (160ml) tomato puree
¾ cup (180ml) water

1. Spoon rice filling evenly into each squid hood. Secure openings with toothpicks. Place squid in single layer in greased ovenproof dish (3 litre/12 cup capacity), pour over combined puree and wine.

2. Bake, uncovered, in moderate oven 15 minutes, turn squid over. Sprinkle with combined breadcrumbs and oil, bake further 15 minutes or until top is lightly browned and squid is tender. Stand 5 minutes, remove toothpicks. Cut squid into rings, serve with cooking liquid.

3. Rice Filling: Heat oil in pan, add onion and garlic, cook, stirring, until onion is soft. Add rice, stir until coated with oil. Stir in spinach, nutmeg, puree and water, simmer, uncovered, stirring occasionally, until all liquid is absorbed; cool.

Serves 8.

■ Recipe can be prepared a day ahead.
■ Storage: Covered, in refrigerator.
■ Freeze: Not suitable.
■ Microwave: Not suitable.

PIQUANT FISH

Psari Savore

4 rainbow trout
plain flour
oil for shallow-frying
1 tablespoon olive oil
2½ tablespoons plain flour, extra
4 cloves garlic, crushed
salt, pepper
¼ cup (60ml) white wine vinegar
1¼ cups (310ml) dry white wine
½ cup (125ml) water
¼ cup (60ml) lemon juice
2 tablespoons fresh rosemary
    leaves

3. Remove pan from heat, gradually stir in combined vinegar, wine, water and juice, cook, stirring, until mixture boils and thickens slightly. Add rosemary, simmer 2 minutes. Serve trout with sauce.

Serves 4.

■ Recipe best made just before serving.
■ Freeze: Not suitable.
■ Microwave: Not suitable.

1. Toss trout in flour, shake away excess flour. Shallow-fry trout in batches in large pan until well browned; transfer to 2 baking dishes. Bake, uncovered, in slow oven 5 minutes.

2. Heat olive oil in clean pan, add extra flour, garlic and salt and pepper to taste. Cook, stirring, until flour is well browned.

China from Home & Garden on the Mall.

Plates and urn from Themelio-Salapatas.

BAKED LEMON AND TOMATO SARDINES

Sartheles Lathoriganes

8 large (about 400g) fresh sardines
3 medium tomatoes, sliced
⅓ cup (80ml) olive oil
2 tablespoons grated lemon rind
2½ tablespoons lemon juice
2 cloves garlic, crushed
2 tablespoons chopped fresh parsley
1 tablespoon chopped fresh oregano

1. Cut heads from sardines and remove entrails. Cut through underside of sardines to backbone; rinse under cold water.

2. Cut backbone through at tail end with scissors without piercing skin. Pull backbone out towards head end to remove. Remove small bones, press sardines flat.

3. Place tomato slices in single layer into 2 x 20cm x 30cm lamington pans. Place sardines, skin side up, over tomatoes, pour over combined oil, rind, juice and garlic; sprinkle with herbs. Bake, uncovered, in moderately hot oven about 7 minutes or until cooked through.

Serves 4.

■ Recipe best made just before serving.
■ Freeze: Not suitable.
■ Microwave: Not suitable.

BAKED CODFISH PATTIES WITH GARLIC SAUCE

Kroketes Bakaliarou me Skorthalia

500g dried salt cod
4 medium potatoes
1 small onion, grated
1 egg, lightly beaten
2 tablespoons milk
2 tablespoons chopped fresh
    flat-leafed parsley
½ teaspoon ground black pepper
2 tablespoons olive oil

GARLIC SAUCE
10 slices (250g) stale white bread
5 cloves garlic, crushed
¼ cup (60ml) olive oil
2 tablespoons lemon juice
1 tablespoon water
2 tablespoons packaged
    ground almonds
salt, pepper

2. Drain cod, place in pan, cover with cold water, simmer, uncovered, 15 minutes; drain, pat dry with absorbent paper. Flake cod finely, remove any skin and bones. Boil, steam or microwave potatoes until tender, mash well.

4. Place patties on lightly greased oven tray, brush with oil, bake in moderately hot oven 10 minutes. Turn patties over, reduce heat to moderate, bake further 20 minutes or until lightly browned. Serve with garlic sauce.

1. Place cod in bowl, cover well with cold water, cover, stand overnight.

3. Combine cod, potatoes, onion, egg, milk, parsley and pepper in bowl. With wet hands, roll ⅓ cup mixture into a ball, flatten slightly, repeat with remaining mixture.

5. Garlic Sauce: Trim crusts from bread. Soak bread in cold water 2 minutes. Drain, squeeze as much water as possible from bread. Combine bread and remaining ingredients with salt and pepper to taste in bowl; mix well.

Makes about 12.

- Codfish patties can be prepared a day ahead. Garlic sauce can be made a day ahead.
- Storage: Covered, separately in refrigerator.
- Freeze: Codfish patties suitable.
- Microwave: Potatoes suitable.

Plate and jug from Themelio-Salapatas; tiles from Country Floors.

SNAPPER CUTLETS WITH TOMATO HERB CRUST

Psari Plaki

¼ cup (60ml) olive oil
1 clove garlic, crushed
2 medium onions, sliced
2 sticks celery, chopped
3 medium tomatoes, peeled, chopped
¾ cup chopped fresh parsley
4 snapper cutlets
1 teaspoon dried oregano leaves
salt, pepper
1 medium lemon, thinly sliced
½ cup (125ml) dry white wine
¼ cup (60ml) lemon juice
¼ cup (15g) stale breadcrumbs

2. Place fish in single layer in baking dish, sprinkle with oregano and salt and pepper to taste. Top with tomato mixture.

1. Heat oil in pan, add garlic, onions and celery, cook, stirring, until onions are soft. Add tomatoes, cook, stirring, until tomatoes are soft; add parsley, mix well.

3. Layer lemon slices over tomato mixture, pour over combined wine and juice, sprinkle with breadcrumbs. Bake, uncovered, in moderate oven about 30 minutes or until fish is tender.

Serves 4.

■ Recipe best made just before serving.
■ Freeze: Not suitable.
■ Microwave: Not suitable.

Urn and box from Themelio-Salapatas; tiles from Country Floors.

OCTOPUS IN RED WINE

Oktapothi Krasato

2kg baby octopus
⅓ cup (80ml) olive oil
2 cloves garlic, crushed
500g baby onions, quartered
2 bay leaves
1½ cups (375ml) dry red wine
1 cup (250ml) water
¼ cup (60ml) red wine vinegar
440ml can tomato puree
1 teaspoon chicken stock powder
2 teaspoons dried oregano leaves
2 teaspoons sugar
salt, pepper
1 tablespoon chopped fresh parsley

2. Heat oil in pan, add octopus and garlic, cook, stirring, until most of the octopus liquid is evaporated.

1. Cut heads from octopus just below eyes, discard heads; remove beaks. Wash octopus; cut into quarters.

3. Add onions, bay leaves, wine, water, vinegar, puree and stock powder. Simmer, uncovered, about 1½ hours or until octopus are tender, stirring occasionally. Remove bay leaves, add oregano, sugar and salt and pepper to taste; mix well. Sprinkle with parsley just before serving.

Serves 4.

■ Recipe can be made a day ahead.
■ Storage: Covered, in refrigerator.
■ Freeze: Not suitable.
■ Microwave: Not suitable.

CHILLED MARINATED FISH WITH CURRANTS

Psari Ksithato

We used perch fillets in this recipe, but any firm white fish fillets are suitable.

1kg firm white fish fillets
⅓ cup (80ml) olive oil
1 medium red Spanish onion,
   finely chopped
3 cloves garlic, crushed
2 medium tomatoes, peeled,
   seeded, chopped
½ cup (125ml) dry white wine
1 tablespoon chopped
   fresh rosemary
1 bay leaf
2 tablespoons currants
½ teaspoon sugar
salt, pepper
½ cup (125ml) white wine vinegar
½ cup (125ml) olive oil, extra

2. Heat remaining oil in pan, add onion and garlic, cook, stirring, until onion is soft. Stir in tomatoes, wine, rosemary, bay leaf, currants and sugar with salt and pepper to taste, simmer, uncovered, about 10 minutes or until thick.

1. Cut each fillet into 3 long, thin pieces. Place fish in baking dish, drizzle with 2 tablespoons of the oil. Bake, uncovered, in moderately hot oven about 15 minutes or until just tender; drain. Transfer fish to shallow glass or ceramic dish.

3. Stir vinegar and extra oil into hot tomato mixture, spoon over warm fish; cool, cover, refrigerate overnight. Remove bay leaf before serving.

Serves 4 to 6.

■ Recipe best made a day ahead.
■ Storage: Covered, in refrigerator.
■ Freeze: Not suitable.
■ Microwave: Not suitable.

VEAL WITH EGGPLANT AND OLIVES

Vithelo me Melitzana ke Elies

1 large eggplant
coarse cooking salt
¼ cup (60ml) olive oil
1 tablespoon olive oil, extra
1kg diced veal
2 medium onions, chopped
2 teaspoons ground cumin
¼ teaspoon ground allspice
½ teaspoon ground cinnamon
½ teaspoon ground coriander
1 teaspoon paprika
¼ teaspoon cayenne pepper
4 cloves garlic, crushed
2 bay leaves
2 x 425g cans tomatoes
¼ cup (60ml) tomato paste
½ cup (125ml) water
1¾ cups (430ml) dry red wine
¼ cup (60ml) lemon juice
½ cup (90g) pitted black
    olives, quartered
½ cup (90g) pimiento-stuffed
    green olives, quartered
2 tablespoons chopped fresh
    flat-leafed parsley
½ teaspoon sugar
salt, pepper

1. Cut eggplant into 2.5cm pieces, sprinkle with salt, stand 30 minutes. Rinse eggplant under cold water, drain, pat dry with absorbent paper.

2. Heat oil in large pan, add eggplant, cook until lightly browned, remove eggplant from pan.

3. Heat extra oil in same pan, add veal in batches, cook until browned all over, remove veal from pan.

4. Add onions to same pan, cook, stirring, until soft. Return veal to pan, add spices, garlic and bay leaves, cook, stirring, 1 minute.

5. Add undrained crushed tomatoes, paste, water and wine, stir until combined, simmer, covered, over low heat 1 hour, stirring occasionally. Add eggplant, simmer, covered, 20 minutes or until eggplant and veal are tender. Add juice, olives, parsley and sugar with salt and pepper to taste, simmer until heated through.

Serves 4 to 6.

- Recipe can be made a day ahead.
- Storage: Covered, in refrigerator.
- Freeze: Not suitable.
- Microwave: Not suitable.

BRAISED VEAL WITH PASTA

Pastitsada

Ask your butcher to roll and tie the veal for you.

1.7kg boned veal shoulder, rolled, tied
salt, pepper
4 cloves garlic, sliced
¼ cup (60ml) olive oil
1 cinnamon stick
2 cloves
1 bay leaf
¼ cup (60ml) red wine vinegar
1 cup (250ml) dry red wine
2 tablespoons olive oil, extra
2 large onions, chopped
2 x 425g cans tomatoes
1 teaspoon sugar
pinch cayenne pepper
250g penne pasta
80g hard goats' cheese, grated

1. Rub veal with salt and pepper. With a sharp knife, make small incisions in veal; insert a slice of garlic in each incision, using half the garlic.

2. Heat oil in large flameproof dish, add veal, cook until browned all over. Add remaining garlic, cinnamon, cloves, bay leaf, vinegar and wine, bring to boil, cover tightly with foil and lid, bake in slow oven 1 hour, turning once.

3. Heat extra oil in pan, add onions, cook, stirring, until soft. Add undrained crushed tomatoes, sugar and cayenne pepper, simmer, uncovered, about 20 minutes or until thickened slightly.

4. Add tomato mixture to veal in dish, cover, bake in moderately slow oven 2 hours, turn veal occasionally. Remove veal from dish, keep warm. Skim fat from tomato mixture, discard cinnamon stick, cloves and bay leaf.

5. Add pasta to pan of boiling water, boil, uncovered, until tender; drain. Meanwhile, simmer tomato mixture about 15 minutes or until thickened and reduced by half; add salt and pepper to taste. You will need about 3½ cups (875ml) tomato sauce for this recipe. Slice veal.

6. Combine pasta, half the tomato sauce and half the cheese in bowl, spread over base of ovenproof dish (2 litre/8 cup capacity). Place veal on top of pasta, pour over remaining tomato sauce, sprinkle with remaining cheese. Bake, covered, in moderately hot oven about 30 minutes or until heated through.

Serves 6 to 8.

- ■ Veal can be baked a day ahead.
- ■ Storage: Covered, in refrigerator.
- ■ Freeze: Cooked veal and tomato sauce suitable.
- ■ Microwave: Pasta suitable.

for buffet parties

ROAST PORK WITH ORANGES AND OLIVES

Hirino Fournou me Portokali ke Elies

2.5kg loin of pork, boned
1 tablespoon olive oil
1 tablespoon honey
1 tablespoon ouzo
1 tablespoon chopped fresh parsley
4 cloves garlic, crushed
salt, pepper
1 cup (160g) pitted black olives

MARINADE
2 medium oranges
2 medium lemons
¾ cup (180ml) orange juice
¼ cup (60ml) lemon juice
1 tablespoon chopped fresh thyme
2 tablespoons honey
⅓ cup (80ml) ouzo

2. Roll pork firmly, secure with string at 2cm intervals. Combine pork and marinade in large shallow dish, cover, refrigerate overnight; turn the pork occasionally in marinade.

4. Add remaining reserved marinade and olives, bake, uncovered, further 10 minutes or until pork is tender. Remove pork and olives, stir pan juices over heat until slightly thickened. Remove string, serve pork with olives and pan juices.

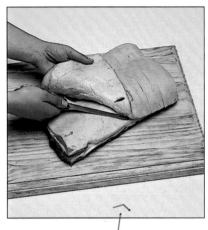

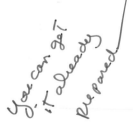

You can get it already prepared.

1. Place pork on bench, skin side up. Run knife 5mm under rind, gradually separating rind from pork. Trim excess fat; discard rind and fat.

3. Remove pork from marinade, reserve marinade. Combine oil, honey, ouzo, parsley, garlic and salt and pepper to taste in bowl; mix well. Place pork in baking dish. Brush honey mixture over pork. Bake, uncovered, in moderately hot oven 1 hour, brushing occasionally with some of the reserved marinade.

5. Marinade: Using vegetable peeler, peel rind from oranges and lemons, cut rind into thin strips. Combine rind, juices, thyme, honey and ouzo in bowl; mix well.

Serves 6. — *8-10*

■ Recipe best marinated a day ahead.
■ Storage: Covered, in refrigerator.
■ Freeze: Uncooked marinated pork suitable.
■ Microwave: Not suitable.

Saucepan from The Bay Tree.

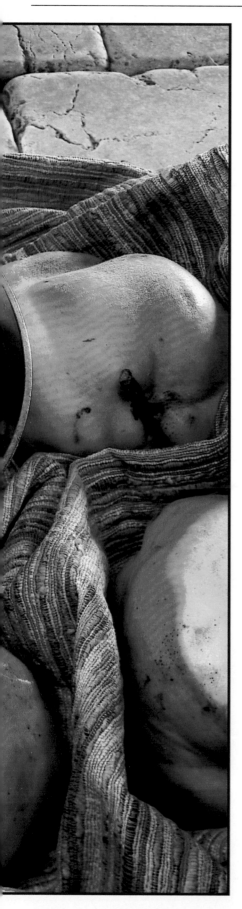

PORK AND QUINCE CASSEROLE

Hirino me Kithonia

1 cup (220g) sugar
2 cups (500ml) water
2 small quince, quartered
⅓ cup (80ml) olive oil
1 large onion, sliced
2 cloves garlic, crushed
1kg diced pork
plain flour
1 cup (250ml) dry red wine
2 cups (500ml) beef stock
1 cinnamon stick
2 strips orange rind
2 tablespoons chopped fresh thyme
salt, pepper

3. Transfer onion mixture and pork to large pan, add combined wine, stock, cinnamon, rind and thyme, simmer, covered, 30 minutes, stirring occasionally.

1. Combine sugar and water in pan, stir over heat, without boiling, until sugar is dissolved. Add quince, simmer, covered, about 5 minutes or until just tender; cool.

4. Drain and chop quince; discard sugar syrup. Add quince with salt and pepper to taste to pork mixture, simmer, covered, further 30 minutes or until pork is tender.

Serves 6.

- Recipe can be made a day ahead.
- Storage: Covered, in refrigerator.
- Freeze: Not suitable.
- Microwave: Not suitable.

2. Heat half the oil in pan, add onion and garlic, cook, stirring, until onion is soft; drain on absorbent paper. Toss pork in flour, shake away excess flour. Heat remaining oil in pan, add pork in batches, cook until lightly browned all over; drain on absorbent paper.

PORK IN GARLIC AND WALNUT SAUCE

Hirino se Saltsa Skorthalias

2 medium red peppers
2 tablespoons olive oil
4 medium pork loin chops
2 cloves garlic, crushed
410g can tomatoes
1 cinnamon stick
¾ cup (180ml) water
¾ cup (180ml) dry white wine
salt, pepper

GARLIC AND WALNUT SAUCE
1 slice white bread
½ cup (60g) chopped walnuts
2 cloves garlic, crushed
¼ cup (60ml) white vinegar

1. Quarter peppers, remove seeds and membranes. Grill peppers skin side up until skin blisters and blackens. Peel away skin, cut peppers into 2cm strips.

2. Heat oil in large pan, add pork in batches, cook until well browned, remove from pan. Add garlic, undrained crushed tomatoes, cinnamon, water and wine to pan, bring to boil. Return pork to pan, add peppers, simmer, covered, about 40 minutes or until pork is tender.

3. Take a little of the hot sauce from pan, stir into garlic and walnut sauce in bowl. Add garlic and walnut sauce to pan, add salt and pepper to taste; stir until heated through. Discard cinnamon.

4. Garlic and Walnut Sauce: Cut crust from bread. Soak bread in cold water 2 minutes. Drain, squeeze as much water as possible from bread. Process walnuts until finely chopped, remove from processor. Process bread, garlic and vinegar until smooth, add to walnuts in bowl; stir until well combined.

Serves 4.

■ Recipe can be made a day ahead.
■ Storage: Covered, in refrigerator.
■ Freeze: Not suitable.
■ Microwave: Not suitable.

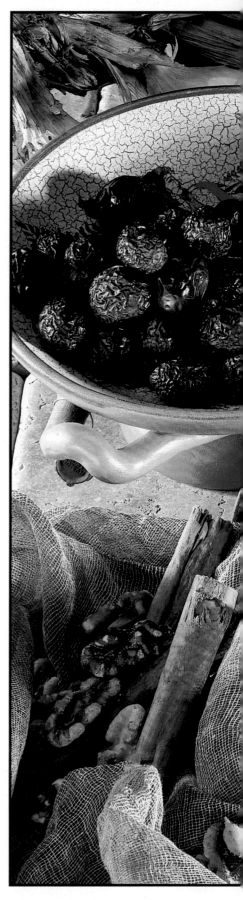

LAMB CABBAGE ROLLS

Dolmathes

12 large cabbage leaves
1 tablespoon olive oil
1 medium onion, chopped
1 clove garlic, crushed
500g minced lamb
¼ cup (50g) long-grain rice
1 small tomato, peeled, chopped
1 tablespoon chopped fresh parsley
1 teaspoon chopped fresh dill
pinch ground cinnamon
salt, pepper
2½ cups (625ml) hot chicken stock
20g butter
2 teaspoons cornflour
2 teaspoons water
1 egg, separated
2 tablespoons lemon juice

2. Heat oil in pan, add onion and garlic, cook, stirring, until onion is soft; cool. Combine onion mixture, mince, rice, tomato, herbs and cinnamon in bowl, add salt and pepper to taste; mix well.

4. Remove rolls from stock; keep warm. Simmer stock, uncovered, until reduced to ½ cup (125ml). Stir in blended cornflour and water, stir over heat until mixture boils and thickens slightly.

3. Divide mince mixture into 12 portions. Place a portion in centre of each cabbage leaf. Fold in sides of leaves and roll up to enclose filling. Place cabbage rolls close together over base of large pan. Pour over stock, dot with butter. Place a plate on top of the rolls to keep the rolls in position during cooking, simmer, covered, over low heat about 1 hour or until the rolls are cooked through.

5. Beat egg white in small bowl with electric mixer until stiff peaks form, beat in egg yolk. Beat in juice and hot stock mixture. Return sauce to pan, whisk over heat until heated through; do not boil. Serve sauce with cabbage rolls.

Makes 12.

■ Cabbage rolls can be made a day ahead. Sauce best made just before serving.
■ Storage: Covered, in refrigerator.
■ Freeze: Uncooked rolls suitable.
■ Microwave: Not suitable.

1. Add leaves in batches to large pan of boiling water, simmer, uncovered, until leaves are soft; drain, pat dry with absorbent paper. Cut any thick core from leaves.

LAMB IN FILLO PARCELS

Arni se Filo

2 tablespoons olive oil
2 (about 450g) lamb
    backstraps, halved
1 tablespoon olive oil, extra
1 medium onion, finely chopped
2 cloves garlic, crushed
425g can tomatoes
2 teaspoons chopped fresh thyme
2 teaspoons chopped fresh rosemary
8 sheets fillo pastry
80g butter, melted
200g feta cheese, crumbled

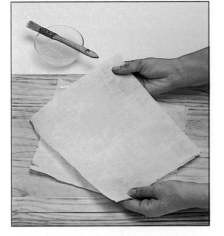

3. To prevent pastry from drying out, cover with a damp tea-towel until you are ready to use it. Layer 2 pastry sheets together, brushing each with some of the butter, cut in half crossways. Layer pieces at an angle on top of each other.

1. Heat oil in pan, add lamb in batches, cook quickly until well browned all over; drain on absorbent paper.

4. Place a piece of lamb in centre of pastry, top with quarter of tomato mixture and quarter of cheese, gather edges together to form a parcel, brush with a little more butter. Repeat with remaining pastry, butter, lamb, tomato mixture and cheese. Place parcels on greased oven tray. Bake, uncovered, in moderate oven about 20 minutes or until browned.

Serves 4.

■ Tomato mixture can be made
   a day ahead.
■ Storage: Covered, in refrigerator.
■ Freeze: Not suitable.
■ Microwave: Not suitable.

2. Add extra oil to pan, add onion, cook, stirring, until onion is soft. Add garlic, un-drained crushed tomatoes and herbs, cook, uncovered, about 10 minutes, stirring occasionally, or until thick; cool.

EGGPLANT MOUSSAKA

Moussaka

2 large (about 1.2kg) eggplants
coarse cooking salt
¼ cup (60ml) olive oil
2 tablespoons olive oil, extra
1 large onion, chopped
2 cloves garlic, crushed
1kg minced lamb
425g can tomatoes
2 tablespoons tomato paste
½ cup (125ml) dry red wine
2 tablespoons chopped fresh parsley
1 teaspoon sugar
¼ teaspoon ground cinnamon
salt, pepper
¼ cup (20g) grated parmesan cheese
½ teaspoon ground nutmeg

CHEESE SAUCE
125g butter
⅔ cup (100g) plain flour
1 litre (4 cups) milk
½ cup (40g) grated parmesan cheese
2 eggs

2. Heat extra oil in pan, add onion and garlic, cook, stirring, until onion is soft. Add mince, cook, stirring, until mince is browned. Add undrained crushed tomatoes, paste, wine, parsley, sugar and cinnamon with salt and pepper to taste, simmer, covered, 30 minutes.

4. Spread cheese sauce over eggplant, sprinkle with cheese and nutmeg. Bake, uncovered, in moderate oven about 45 minutes or until lightly browned.

1. Cut eggplants into 5mm slices, sprinkle with salt, stand 20 minutes. Rinse eggplant under cold water; drain, pat dry with absorbent paper. Place eggplant slices in single layer on lightly greased oven trays. Brush with oil, grill on both sides until lightly browned; drain on absorbent paper.

3. Grease ovenproof dish (2.5 litre/10 cup capacity). Line dish with one-third of the eggplant, top with half the meat sauce, then half the remaining eggplant, remaining meat sauce and remaining eggplant.

5. Cheese Sauce: Melt butter in pan, stir in flour, stir over heat until bubbling. Remove from heat, gradually stir in milk, stir over heat until mixture boils and thickens. Remove from heat, stir in cheese, cool slightly, stir in eggs; mix until smooth.

Serves 6.

■ Recipe can be made a day ahead.
■ Storage: Covered, in refrigerator.
■ Freeze: Suitable.
■ Microwave: Not suitable.

ROAST GARLIC LAMB WITH LEMON POTATOES

Arni Lemonato me Patates

½ cup (125ml) olive oil
2 tablespoons grated lemon rind
2 tablespoons lemon juice
2 tablespoons dry white wine
2 teaspoons seasoned pepper
2 tablespoons chopped fresh thyme
2kg leg of lamb
2 cloves garlic, sliced
1 tablespoon fresh rosemary leaves

LEMON POTATOES
12 medium old potatoes
¼ cup (60ml) olive oil
⅓ cup (80ml) lemon juice
1½ tablespoons grated lemon rind
2 tablespoons chopped
    fresh rosemary
2 tablespoons chopped fresh thyme
1½ teaspoons cracked
    black peppercorns
salt

1. Combine oil, rind, juice, wine, pepper and thyme in jug; mix well. Trim excess fat from lamb. Using point of knife, make 12 incisions evenly over top of lamb leg. Place a slice of garlic and some of the rosemary leaves in each incision. Pour oil mixture over lamb, cover, refrigerate, turning lamb occasionally, for 3 hours or overnight.

2. Drain lamb, reserve marinade. Place lamb in large baking dish, bake, uncovered, in moderately hot oven 40 minutes. Add lemon potatoes, bake further 50 minutes, turning occasionally, or until lamb and potatoes are tender.

3. Remove lamb from baking dish, cover, keep warm. Drain juices from pan; reserve juices. Return potatoes to very hot oven, bake further 20 minutes or until potatoes are browned and crisp. Heat reserved marinade and reserved juices in pan, bring to boil, serve with sliced lamb and lemon potatoes.

4. **Lemon Potatoes:** Cut potatoes into 3cm pieces, place in bowl, pour over combined remaining ingredients; mix well.
Serves 6.

- ▪ Lamb can be made a day ahead.
- ▪ Storage: Covered, in refrigerator.
- ▪ Freeze: Not suitable.
- ▪ Microwave: Not suitable.

Glasses, plate and jug from Morris Home & Garden Wares.

GARLIC AND LEMON LAMB KEBABS

Souvlakia

1.5kg lamb leg steaks
3 medium lemons
1 cup (250ml) lemon juice
8 cloves garlic, crushed
¼ cup chopped fresh
    rosemary leaves
1 tablespoon seasoned pepper
2 tablespoons mild mustard
½ cup (125ml) olive oil
2 tablespoons olive oil, extra
30g butter

1. Cut lamb into 3cm pieces. Using vegetable peeler, peel rind thinly from lemons, cut rind into thin strips. Combine lamb and rind in large bowl, pour over combined juice, garlic, rosemary, pepper, mustard and oil, mix well; cover, refrigerate overnight.

2. Drain lamb from marinade; reserve marinade. Thread lamb onto 16 skewers. Heat extra oil in baking dish, add kebabs in batches, cook, turning occasionally, until lightly browned.

3. Return kebabs to baking dish, pour over reserved marinade, bake, uncovered, in moderate oven about 15 minutes or until tender.

4. Remove kebabs from baking dish, boil marinade in dish, uncovered, until reduced to 1½ cups (375ml), add butter, stir until melted. Serve sauce with kebabs.

Makes 16.

■ Recipe best prepared a day ahead.
■ Storage: Covered, in refrigerator.
■ Freeze: Uncooked marinated
    lamb suitable.
■ Microwave: Not suitable.

FRICASSEE OF LAMB WITH LETTUCE

Arni Frikase

¼ cup (60ml) olive oil
12 lamb neck chops
3 medium onions, finely chopped
4 cloves garlic, crushed
1 tablespoon grated lemon rind
3 cups (750ml) chicken stock
2 tablespoons honey
3 bay leaves
salt, pepper
1 large iceberg lettuce, shredded
¼ cup chopped fresh mint
¼ cup chopped fresh parsley
2 eggs
⅓ cup (80ml) lemon juice

3. Add lettuce and herbs, cook, stirring, until lettuce is just wilted.

1. Heat oil in pan, add lamb chops in batches, cook until lightly browned all over; drain on absorbent paper.

2. Add onions, garlic and rind to same pan, cook, stirring, until onions are soft. Return lamb to pan, pour over stock, honey, bay leaves and salt and pepper to taste. Simmer, covered, about 1¾ hours or until lamb is tender.

4. Beat eggs in small bowl with electric mixer until thick, gradually add juice, beat until combined. Add egg mixture to lamb, stir until heated through; do not boil. Remove bay leaves before serving.

Serves 4 to 6.

▪ Recipe can be prepared a day ahead up to the end of step 2.
▪ Storage: Covered, in refrigerator.
▪ Freeze: Not suitable.
▪ Microwave: Not suitable.

GOAT AND HARICOT BEAN CASSEROLE

Katsiki Kokkinisto me Fasolia

You will need to order goat from a specialist Continental butcher; however, the casserole is equally delicious with lamb.

2 cups (400g) dried haricot beans
2kg leg of goat, butterflied
¼ cup (60ml) olive oil
2 medium onions, chopped
2 cloves garlic, crushed
2 x 425g cans tomatoes
¼ cup (60ml) tomato paste
½ cup (125ml) dry red wine
1 cinnamon stick
1 tablespoon lemon juice
2 tablespoons chopped fresh parsley
salt, pepper

1. Place beans in bowl, cover well with cold water, cover, stand overnight. Drain beans, add to pan of boiling water, simmer, uncovered, about 30 minutes or until tender; drain well.

2. Cut goat into 3cm pieces. Heat oil in pan, add goat in batches, cook until well browned; remove from pan. Add onions and garlic to same pan, cook, stirring, until onions are soft; return goat to pan.

3. Stir in undrained crushed tomatoes, paste, wine and cinnamon, simmer, covered, about 2 hours or until goat is tender, stirring occasionally.

4. Add beans, juice and parsley with salt and pepper to taste to pan, stir over heat until heated through. Discard cinnamon stick before serving.

Serves 6.

- Recipe can be made a day before serving.
- Storage: Covered, in refrigerator.
- Freeze: Suitable.
- Microwave: Not suitable.

TREATS & SWEETS

ZAHAROPLASTIKI

Although fresh fruit is probably the only true dessert in Greece, there is a delicious tradition of treats and sweets to serve with coffee, often after a meal, and always when visitors come to the home. In our selection, you can sample luscious syrup-soaked cakes and rich, nutty pastries, Easter bread with red-dyed eggs, glace orange peel rolls and lots more. Most can be made ahead, ready for any occasion.

HONEY COOKIES

Melomakarona

125g butter
2 teaspoons grated lemon rind
⅓ cup (75g) castor sugar
⅓ cup (80ml) oil
2 cups (300g) plain flour
1 cup (150g) self-raising flour
¼ cup (30g) chopped walnuts
⅔ cup (160ml) orange juice
1 cup (250ml) honey
2 tablespoons chopped walnuts, extra
2 teaspoons sesame seeds

2. Transfer mixture to large bowl, stir in sifted flours, nuts and juice in 2 batches, mix to a soft dough.

4. Heat honey in pan until just warm, dip biscuits in honey to coat, place on wire rack over tray, sprinkle with combined extra nuts and seeds.

Makes about 40.

■ Recipe can be made 2 days ahead.
■ Storage: Airtight container.
■ Freeze: Undipped biscuits suitable.
■ Microwave: Not suitable.

1. Cream butter, rind and sugar in small bowl with electric mixer until combined. Gradually beat in oil, beat until mixture is light and fluffy.

3. Roll level tablespoons of mixture into egg shapes, place on lightly greased oven trays, flatten slightly. Mark biscuits lightly with fork. Bake in moderate oven about 20 minutes or until browned. Stand biscuits on oven trays 5 minutes before placing on wire rack to cool.

NEW YEAR CAKE

Vasilopita

Part of the Greek New Year tradition is to bake a Vasilopita; the name is derived from St Basil, the patron saint of wishes and blessings, whose feast day is celebrated then. A coin is traditionally put into the cake, and means good luck to the recipient. All the family join in around the cake, embracing warmly and sharing good wishes, then the cake is cut.

250g butter
2 teaspoons grated lemon rind
2½ cups (550g) castor sugar
6 eggs
1 cup (150g) self-raising flour
2 cups (300g) plain flour
½ teaspoon bicarbonate of soda
1 cup (250ml) milk
2 tablespoons lemon juice
¼ cup (35g) pistachios, chopped
¼ cup (35g) walnuts, chopped
**¼ cup (40g) blanched
    almonds, chopped**

TOPPING
¼ cup (35g) pistachios
¼ cup (35g) walnuts, chopped
¼ cup (35g) slivered almonds
¼ cup (55g) sugar

1. Lightly grease deep 28cm round cake pan, line base with paper, grease paper. Cream butter and rind in small bowl with electric mixer until light in colour. Add sugar, beat until light and fluffy. Gradually add eggs 1 at a time, beating well between each addition.

2. Transfer butter mixture to large bowl, stir in sifted flours and soda, and milk in 2 batches. Stir in juice and nuts.

3. Pour mixture into prepared pan, bake in moderate oven 30 minutes. Remove cake from oven, sprinkle with topping, press on lightly. Bake about further 40 minutes. Stand cake 5 minutes in pan, turn onto wire rack covered with greaseproof paper, turn cake over; cool.

4. Topping: Combine all ingredients in bowl; mix well.

■ Recipe can be made a day ahead.
■ Storage: Airtight container.
■ Freeze: Not suitable.
■ Microwave: Not suitable.

Plate from Morris Home & Garden Wares; carafe and glasses from Montague North; rug from Zante Imports.

THIPLES

Thiples

The pretty shapes of these bubbly fried pastries can vary; they are usually made for celebrations.

2 cups (300g) plain flour, approximately
3 eggs
cornflour
oil for shallow-frying
⅔ cup (160ml) honey
2 tablespoons sesame seeds
1 teaspoon ground cinnamon

1. Sift 1¾ cups (260g) of the flour into bowl. Beat eggs in small bowl with electric mixer until thick and pale. Add eggs to flour in bowl, stir until mixture forms a stiff dough; bring dough together with hand.

2. Turn dough onto lightly floured surface, knead about 10 minutes or until dough becomes smooth, sprinkling with a little more of the remaining flour if dough becomes sticky. Divide dough into 8 equal portions, cover with plastic wrap. Lightly dust surface with cornflour. Roll a portion of dough into 50cm strip about .5mm thick (number 7 on pasta machine). Using pastry wheel, trim edges and cut dough into 2 x 5cm x 50cm strips. Discard scraps.

3. Pinch opposite sides of a strip together at 7cm intervals. Starting from 1 end, gently turn strip to form a large round, pinching ends where pastry meets to secure round; moisten ends lightly with water to seal. Repeat with remaining strip.

4. Place thiples top side down in hot oil, shallow-fry until puffed and pale, turn to cook other side; drain on absorbent paper. Make and cook thiples in batches, using 1 portion of dough at a time. Just before serving, drizzle thiples with honey, sprinkle with seeds and cinnamon.

Makes 16.

■ Thiples can be made a week ahead.
■ Storage: Airtight container.
■ Freeze: Suitable.
■ Microwave: Not suitable.

HALVA

Halva

125g butter
1 cup (160g) semolina
2 tablespoons slivered almonds
2½ cups (625ml) water
1 cup (220g) castor sugar
1 teaspoon ground cinnamon

1. Heat butter in pan, add semolina and nuts, cook, stirring constantly, about 5 minutes or until semolina is lightly browned. Remove pan from heat.

2. Combine water and sugar in pan, stir over heat without boiling, until sugar is dissolved. Bring to boil, simmer, uncovered, without stirring, 5 minutes. Gradually stir hot syrup into semolina mixture, add cinnamon, stir over low heat until smooth and bubbling; cook, stirring, further 2 minutes.

3. Remove from heat, cover pan with folded tea-towel, then lid; stand 15 minutes.

Mugs and rug from Zante Imports.

4. Grease base of 20cm round cake pan, cover base with baking paper, grease paper. Spread mixture evenly into pan. Place pan on wire rack, stand 5 minutes, turn halva onto serving plate. Cut into wedges to serve.

■ Recipe can be made 2 days ahead.
■ Storage: Covered, in refrigerator.
■ Freeze: Not suitable.
■ Microwave: Not suitable.

EASTER BREAD

Tsoureki Paschalino

This is one of various breads baked during Holy Week, the week before Easter, ready for the traditional midnight supper on Easter Sunday morning after the Resurrection Service. The 3 dough ropes plaited together symbolise the Holy Trinity; the red eggs symbolise the blood shed by Christ. For our eggs, we used a special Greek red dye available at Continental delicatessens.

3 teaspoons (10g) dried yeast
⅓ cup (75g) castor sugar
1 cup (250ml) warm milk
3½ cups (525g) plain flour
1 teaspoon salt
1½ teaspoons ground allspice
½ teaspoon ground cinnamon
90g butter, melted
2 eggs, lightly beaten
2 teaspoons grated lemon rind
1 egg, lightly beaten, extra
1 tablespoon finely chopped
    blanched almonds

RED-DYED EGGS
½ teaspoon Greek red food dye
1 cup (250ml) white vinegar
½ cup (125ml) warm water
4 eggs

1. Combine yeast, 2 teaspoons of the sugar and milk in small bowl, cover, stand in warm place about 10 minutes or until mixture is frothy. Sift flour, salt and spices into large bowl, stir in remaining sugar and combined yeast mixture, butter, eggs and rind, mix to a soft dough.

2. Turn dough onto lightly floured surface, knead about 10 minutes or until smooth and elastic.

3. Place dough in lightly oiled bowl, cover, stand in warm place about 1 hour or until dough is doubled in size.

4. Knead dough on lightly floured surface until smooth. Divide dough into 3 pieces, roll into 60cm strands. Plait strands, place on lightly greased oven tray, shape into 24cm ring, pinch ends to seal.

5. Press red-dyed eggs firmly around ring at 6cm intervals. Cover, stand in warm place about 40 minutes or until dough is almost doubled in size. Brush with extra egg, sprinkle with nuts. Bake in moderately hot oven 10 minutes, reduce heat to moderate, bake about further 25 minutes or until browned.

6. Red-Dyed Eggs: Combine dye, vinegar and warm water in jug, stir to dissolve dye. Wash eggs well, place in pan, cover with cold water. Bring to boil, pour in dye mixture, boil 10 minutes. Remove eggs from pan; cool. Polish eggs with lightly oiled cloth before using.

▪ Recipe can be made a day ahead.
▪ Storage: Airtight container.
▪ Freeze: Not suitable.
▪ Microwave: Not suitable.

YOGURT CAKE

Yiaourtopita

125g butter
1 cup (220g) castor sugar
3 eggs, separated
2 cups (300g) self-raising flour
½ teaspoon bicarbonate of soda
¼ cup (25g) finely chopped
   blanched almonds
1 cup (250ml) plain yogurt
icing sugar

3. Beat egg whites in small bowl with electric mixer until soft peaks form. Gently fold egg whites into yogurt mixture in 2 batches. Spread mixture into prepared pan, bake in moderate oven about 35 minutes. Turn cake onto wire rack to cool; dust with sifted icing sugar.

■ Recipe best made on day of serving.
■ Freeze: Suitable.
■ Microwave: Not suitable.

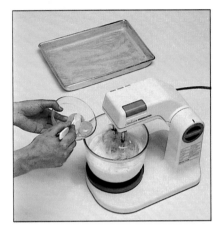

1. Lightly grease 20cm x 30cm lamington pan, line base and sides with paper, grease paper. Cream butter and sugar in small bowl with electric mixer until light and fluffy. Add egg yolks 1 at a time, beating well between additions.

2. Transfer mixture to large bowl, stir in sifted flour and soda in 2 batches, add nuts and yogurt; stir until smooth.

BAKLAVA CIGARS

Poura

1½ cups (150g) walnuts,
  finely chopped
½ cup (80g) blanched almonds,
  finely chopped
¼ cup (55g) castor sugar
1 teaspoon ground cinnamon
½ teaspoon ground cloves
10 sheets fillo pastry
150g unsalted butter, melted
1 tablespoon blanched almonds,
  finely chopped, extra
¼ teaspoon ground cinnamon, extra

SYRUP
1 lemon
1 cup (220g) castor sugar
1 cup (250ml) water
1 cinnamon stick
2 cloves

3. Place cigars in single layer in shallow pan, pour over warm syrup, cool to room temperature. Sprinkle with extra nuts and extra cinnamon.

4. Syrup: Using vegetable peeler, peel rind thinly from half the lemon. Combine sugar and water in pan, stir over heat, without boiling, until sugar is dissolved. Add rind, cinnamon and cloves to pan, simmer, uncovered, without stirring, 2 minutes; cool slightly.

Makes about 30.

- Cigars, without syrup, can be made a week ahead.
- Storage: Airtight container.
- Freeze: Uncooked cigars suitable.
- Microwave: Not suitable.

1. Combine nuts, sugar and spices in bowl.

2. Cover pastry with damp tea-towel to prevent drying out until you are ready to use it. Cut 1 sheet of pastry crossways into 3 even strips, brush each strip with butter. Spoon 3 level teaspoons of nut mixture into a pile on 1 end of each strip, leaving a 3.5cm border. Fold in sides, brush with butter, roll up tightly to form a cigar shape. Repeat with remaining pastry, butter and nut mixture. Place cigars onto greased oven trays, brush with remaining butter, bake in moderate oven about 12 minutes or until lightly browned; cool on trays.

China from Corso de Fiori.

GRAPEFRUIT MARMALADE

Marmelatha Frapa

3 medium (about 1kg) grapefruit
3½ cups (875ml) water
4 cups (880g) castor sugar,
   approximately
¼ cup (60ml) strained lemon juice

1. Peel rind with thick pith from grapefruit, cut rind into thin strips. Reserve flesh for another use. Combine rind and water in bowl, cover, stand overnight.

2. Add undrained rind mixture to wide, heavy-based pan, simmer, covered, about 45 minutes or until rind is soft.

3. Measure rind mixture, allow 1 cup of sugar to each cup of mixture. Return rind mixture and sugar to pan, stir over heat, without boiling, until sugar is dissolved.

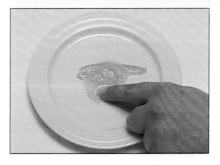

4. Add juice, simmer, uncovered, without stirring, about 15 minutes or until marmalade jells when tested. Pour into hot sterilised jars, seal while hot.

Makes about 1 litre (4 cups).

■ Recipe can be made 3 months ahead.
■ Storage: Cool, dark place. Refrigerate after opening.
■ Freeze: Not suitable.
■ Microwave: Not suitable.

SEMOLINA CAKE

Revani

4 eggs, separated
⅓ cup (75g) castor sugar
½ teaspoon vanilla essence
1 teaspoon grated orange rind
1½ tablespoons ouzo
⅓ cup (80ml) fresh orange juice
½ cup (80g) semolina
⅓ cup (55g) blanched
    almonds, chopped

SYRUP
1 lemon
1 cup (220g) castor sugar
1 cup (250ml) water
1 teaspoon lemon juice

1. Lightly grease 23cm square slab cake pan. Beat egg yolks, sugar, essence and rind in small bowl with electric mixer until light and fluffy. Gradually add ouzo, beat until just combined.

2. Transfer mixture to large bowl, stir in orange juice, semolina and nuts; cover, stand for 30 minutes.

3. Beat egg whites in small bowl with electric mixer until firm peaks form, fold gently into cake mixture in 2 batches.

4. Pour mixture into prepared pan, bake in moderately hot oven about 20 minutes. Pour warm syrup over warm cake in pan; cool. Cut cold cake into squares to serve.

5. Syrup: Using vegetable peeler, peel rind thinly from lemon, cut rind into thin strips. Combine sugar, water, juice and rind in pan, stir over heat, without boiling, until sugar is dissolved, simmer, uncovered, without stirring, 5 minutes, cool slightly before using.

- Recipe can be made a day ahead.
- Storage: Covered, in refrigerator.
- Freeze: Not suitable.
- Microwave: Not suitable.

Plate from Accoutrement.

Spoon from Corso de Fiori.

BAKED QUINCE

Kithonia sto Fourno

4 small quince
⅔ cup (160ml) honey, approximately
ground cinnamon

1. Wipe quince with damp cloth, prick skins all over with skewer.

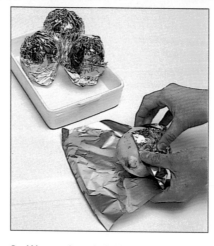

2. Wrap quince individually in foil, place upright, close together in ovenproof dish. Bake in moderately hot oven about 1½ hours or until tender. Cut quince in half, drizzle with honey, sprinkle with cinnamon.

Serves 4.
■ Recipe best made just before serving.
■ Freeze: Not suitable.
■ Microwave: Not suitable.

HONEY WALNUT PUFFS

Loukoumathes

2 teaspoons (7g) dried yeast
1 cup (250ml) warm milk
2 tablespoons castor sugar
1 egg, lightly beaten
60g butter, melted
2 cups (300g) plain flour
oil for deep-frying
2/3 cup (160ml) honey
1/4 teaspoon ground cinnamon
1/4 cup (30g) chopped walnuts

2. Stand, covered, in a warm place about 1½ hours or until batter doubles in size and bubbles appear on the surface. Beat batter until smooth.

4. Heat honey in pan until just warm. Place puffs on serving plate, drizzle with honey, sprinkle with cinnamon and nuts.

Makes about 26.

- ■ Recipe best made just before serving.
- ■ Freeze: Not suitable.
- ■ Microwave: Not suitable.

1. Combine yeast, milk, sugar, egg and butter in large bowl; mix well. Gradually stir in sifted flour; beat until smooth.

3. Deep-fry level tablespoons of batter in hot oil, turning puffs to give an even colour; drain on absorbent paper.

Plates and blue pots from Morris Home & Garden Wares.

GLACE ORANGE PEEL ROLLS

Glyko Portokali

A visitor to a Greek home is traditionally made welcome with a spoon sweet or preserve, such as these orange peel rolls. After about 10 or 15 minutes of conversation, spoon sweets are served to each person with a glass of water. Usually, coffee and a small glass of cognac or liqueur will follow.

**6 large thick-skinned oranges
1.32kg (6 cups) sugar
1.5 litres (6 cups) water
2 tablespoons lemon juice**

3. Place rolls in pan of cold water, bring to boil, drain immediately. Repeat boiling and draining process twice more. Cover rolls again with cold water in pan, bring to boil, simmer, uncovered, about 40 minutes or until tender; drain. Place rolls on wire rack to dry.

4. Combine sugar and the 6 cups of water in large pan, stir over heat, without boiling, until sugar is dissolved; stir in juice. Simmer, uncovered, 5 minutes. Add orange rolls, simmer, uncovered, 10 minutes; cool.

1. Grate oranges lightly. Cut peel lengthways into 6 segments; remove peel. Reserve orange flesh for another use.

2. Roll each segment tightly. Push a needle and strong thread through each roll until 12 rolls are threaded; tie ends together securely. Repeat rolling and threading with remaining peel.

5. Bring rolls to boil, simmer, uncovered, about 50 minutes or until syrup is thickened slightly. Remove thread from rolls. Place rolls in hot sterilised jars, pour over strained syrup; seal while hot.

Makes about 1.75 litres (7 cups).

- Recipe can be made 2 months ahead.
- Storage: Cool, dark place.
- Freeze: Not suitable.
- Microwave: Not suitable.

Dishes from Montague North.

RICE PUDDING

Rizogalo

1 litre (4 cups) milk
⅓ cup (75g) castor sugar
5cm piece orange rind
½ cup (100g) short-grain rice
1 tablespoon custard powder
¼ cup (60ml) milk, extra
ground cinnamon

2. Bring to boil, add rice, simmer, uncovered, about 30 minutes or until rice is tender, stirring occasionally.

1. Combine milk, sugar and orange rind in pan, stir constantly over heat, without boiling, until sugar is dissolved.

3. Remove rind, stir in blended custard powder and extra milk, stir over heat until mixture boils and thickens. Pour mixture into 4 serving dishes, sprinkle with cinnamon. Serve warm or cold.

Serves 4.

- Recipe can be made a day ahead.
- Storage: Covered, in refrigerator.
- Freeze: Not suitable.
- Microwave: Suitable.

ALMOND PEARS

Amigthalota

3 cups (480g) blanched almonds
¾ cup (165g) castor sugar
½ cup (80g) semolina, approximately
3 egg whites, lightly beaten
2 tablespoons orange flower water
35 cloves, approximately
icing sugar

1. Process nuts until fine, transfer nuts to bowl, stir in castor sugar, semolina, egg whites and orange flower water, mix to a smooth, stiff paste. Add a little extra semolina if the paste is too sticky.

3. Transfer almond pears to shallow tray covered with greaseproof paper, dust heavily with sifted icing sugar while warm.

Makes about 35.

- Recipe can be made a month ahead.
- Storage: Airtight container.
- Freeze: Not suitable.
- Microwave: Not suitable.

2. Shape level tablespoons of almond mixture into pear shapes, insert a clove in top of each pear. Place on lightly greased oven trays, bake in moderate oven about 12 minutes or until lightly coloured.

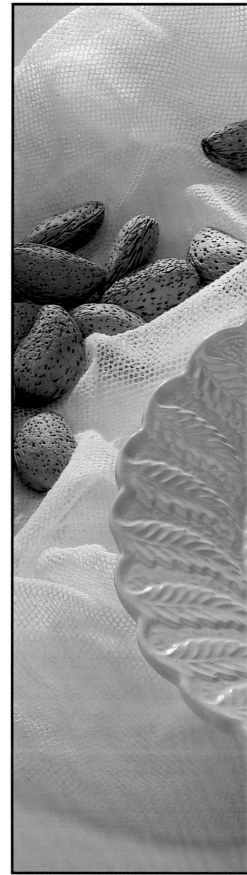

CUSTARD SLICE

Galaktoboureko

¼ cup (40g) semolina
1½ cups (330g) castor sugar
¼ cup (35g) cornflour
6 eggs, lightly beaten
1 teaspoon grated lemon rind
1 litre (4 cups) milk
½ cup (80g) semolina, extra
12 sheets fillo pastry
125g ghee, melted

SYRUP
1 medium lemon
1½ cups (330g) castor sugar
¾ cup (180ml) water
1 cinnamon stick

1. Combine semolina, sugar, cornflour, eggs and rind in bowl, whisk until thick and combined. Bring milk to boil in pan, gradually whisk hot milk into egg mixture. Return mixture to pan.

2. Stir over heat until mixture begins to thicken, gradually add extra semolina, stir until thick, do not boil; cool slightly.

3. Lightly grease 22cm x 30cm ovenproof dish (2.5 litre/10 cup capacity). Cover pastry with damp tea-towel to prevent drying out until you are ready to use it. Brush a pastry sheet with ghee, place into dish so that edges overhang sides. Repeat with 5 more pastry sheets and ghee, allowing pastry to overhang opposite sides of dish.

4. Pour custard mixture evenly into pastry case. Layer remaining sheets of pastry with ghee, place on top of custard, trim overlapping edges of pastry, fold ends inside dish to enclose filling.

5. Brush with remaining ghee. Using sharp knife, score pastry diagonally, cutting through only 1 layer of pastry. Bake in moderate oven about 45 minutes or until custard is set. Pour cold syrup evenly over hot slice; cool in dish before cutting.

6. **Syrup:** Using a vegetable peeler, peel rind thinly from half the lemon. Combine sugar and water in pan, stir over heat without boiling, until sugar is dissolved. Add rind and cinnamon, simmer, uncovered, without stirring, 2 minutes. Cool, discard rind and cinnamon.

Serves 8 to 10.

■ Recipe can be made 2 days ahead.
■ Storage: Covered, in refrigerator.
■ Freeze: Not suitable.
■ Microwave: Not suitable.

Plate from Accoutrement.

MARMALADE SHORTBREAD

Thipla Biscota me Marmelatha

125g butter
1 teaspoon vanilla essence
⅓ cup (75g) castor sugar
2 eggs
½ cup (125ml) oil
3 cups (450g) self-raising flour
½ cup (125ml) marmalade
icing sugar

1. Lightly grease 20cm x 30cm lamington pan, cover base with paper, grease paper. Cream butter, essence and castor sugar in small bowl with electric mixer until light and fluffy. Beat in eggs 1 at a time, beat until combined. Add oil gradually in a thin stream while motor is operating, beat until thick and creamy.

2. Transfer mixture to large bowl, stir in sifted flour in 2 batches.

3. Press dough into prepared pan, mark into squares or rectangles using knife. Bake in moderately slow oven about 20 minutes or until lightly coloured. Cut shortbread into squares or rectangles while warm; cool shortbread in pan.

4. Split shortbread, sandwich with a little marmalade; dust with sifted icing sugar.

Makes about 36.

- Recipe can be made 2 days ahead.
- Storage: Airtight container.
- Freeze: Suitable.
- Microwave: Not suitable.

GLOSSARY

Here are some terms, names and alternatives to help everyone use and

understand our recipes perfectly.

ALCOHOL: is optional, but gives a particular flavour. Use fruit juice or water instead to make up the liquid content required.

ALLSPICE: pimento.

ALMONDS:

Blanched: nuts with skin removed.

Ground: we used packaged commercially ground nuts unless otherwise specified.

Slivered: nuts cut lengthways.

BACON RASHERS: bacon slices.

BEANS:

Haricot: small, white, oval beans with a smooth texture and bland flavour. Require soaking.

BEEF:

Corned silverside: is cut from the outside portion of the upper leg and cured.

Minced beef: ground beef.

Round steak: boneless piece of meat from the upper back leg.

Rump steak: boneless piece of meat that covers the hip bone.

BEETROOT: regular round beet.

BICARBONATE OF SODA: baking soda.

BRANDY: spirit distilled from wine.

BREADCRUMBS:

Packaged: use fine packaged breadcrumbs.

Stale: use 1 or 2-day-old bread made into crumbs by grating, blending or processing.

BUTTER: use salted or unsalted (also called sweet) butter; 125g is equal to 1 stick butter.

CHEESE:

Feta: a soft Greek cheese with a sharp, salty taste.

Hard goats': is made from goats' milk and has a pronounced earthy taste.

Parmesan: sharp-tasting hard cheese used as a flavour accent. We prefer to use fresh parmesan cheese, although it is available already finely grated.

Ricotta: a fresh, unripened light curd cheese.

CHICKEN: size is determined by a numbering system; for example, No 13 is a 1.3kg bird; No 10 is 1kg. This system applies to most poultry.

Breast fillets: skinless and boneless.

Thigh cutlets: have skin and 1 bone; are sometimes called chicken chops.

CHICK PEAS: garbanzos.

CORIANDER: also known as cilantro and Chinese parsley; its seeds are the main ingredient of curry powder. A strongly flavoured herb, use it sparingly until accustomed to the unique flavour. Available fresh, ground and in seed form.

CORNFLOUR: cornstarch.

CRACKED WHEAT: also known as burghul; is wheat which has been cracked by boiling, then dried. It is most often used in Middle Eastern cooking.

CREAM: light pouring cream, also known as half-and-half.

CURRANTS: small dried seedless grapes.

CUSTARD POWDER: pudding mix.

EGGPLANT: aubergine.

ENGLISH SPINACH: a soft-leaved vegetable, more delicate in taste than silverbeet; young silverbeet can be substituted for English spinach.

ESSENCE: extract. We used imitation vanilla essence.

FENNEL: has a slight aniseed taste when fresh, ground or in seed form. Fennel seeds are a component of curry powder. The bulb is eaten uncooked in salads or may be braised, steamed or stir-fried in savoury dishes.

FILLO PASTRY: also known as phyllo dough; comes in tissue-thin pastry sheets bought chilled or frozen.

FLOUR:

White plain: unbleached all-purpose flour.

White self-raising: substitute plain (all-purpose) flour and baking powder in the proportions of 1 cup (150g) plain flour to 2 level teaspoons baking powder. Sift together several times before using.

GHEE: a pure butter fat available in cans, it can be heated to high temperatures without burning because of the lack of salts and milk solids.

GLOBE ARTICHOKE: large flower head of a plant of the thistle family.

GREEN SHALLOTS: also known as scallions and green onions. Do not confuse with the small golden shallots.

LAMB:

Backstrap: the larger fillet from a row of loin chops or cutlets.

Fry: lamb's liver.

Minced: ground lamb.

Shank: portion of front or back leg with bone in.

LENTILS: dried pulses. There are many different varieties, usually identified and named after their colour.

LETTUCE:

Cos: also known as romaine; has crisp, elongated leaves.

Iceberg: is a heavy, firm, round lettuce with tightly packed leaves and crisp texture.

LOBSTER: crayfish.

MORTADELLA: a delicately spiced and smoked cooked sausage made of pork and beef.

MUSHROOMS:

Button: small, unopened mushrooms with a delicate flavour.

Flat: large, soft, flat mushrooms with a rich earthy flavour.

MUSSELS: should be bought from a fish market where there is reliably fresh fish. They must be tightly closed when bought, indicating they are alive. Before cooking, scrub the shells with a strong brush and remove the "beards". Discard shells that do not open after cooking.

OIL: polyunsaturated vegetable oil.

Olive: virgin oil is obtained only from the pulp of high-grade fruit. Pure olive oil is pressed from the pulp and kernels of second grade olives. Extra virgin olive oil is the purest quality virgin oil.

OKRA: a green, ridged, immature seed pod, also called lady's fingers.

OUZO: aniseed-flavoured Greek spirit.

PAPRIKA: ground dried peppers.

PARSLEY, FLAT-LEAFED: also known as continental parsley or Italian parsley.

PEPPERS: capsicum or bell peppers.

PINE NUTS: small, cream-coloured soft kernels.

PISTACHIOS: small oval nuts with a green kernel.

PORK:

Diced: chopped pork.

Loin: from pork middle.

PRAWNS: shrimp.

QUAIL: small game birds from about 250g to 300g.

QUINCE: yellow-skinned fruit with hard texture and acid taste.

RABBIT:

Pieces: jointed rabbit.

RAINBOW TROUT: popular fish with cream pink flesh; is a member of the same family as salmon.

RICE:

White: is hulled and polished, can be short or long-grained.

RIND: zest.

SALT COD: dried salted cod, also known as baccala.

SARDINES: small silvery fish with soft, oily flesh.

SCALLOPS: we used the scallops with coral (roe) attached.

SEASONED PEPPER: a combination of black pepper, sugar and bell pepper.

SEMOLINA: a hard part of the wheat which is sifted out and used mainly for making pasta.

SILVERBEET: also known as Swiss chard. Remove coarse white stems; cook green leafy parts as required by recipes.

SKEWERS: Use metal or bamboo skewers. Rub oil onto metal skewers to stop meat sticking. Soak bamboo skewers in water for at least 1 hour or overnight to stop skewers burning.

SNAPPER CUTLET: crossways slice of fish with bones.

SQUID HOODS: convenient cleaned squid (calamari).

STOCK: 1 cup (250ml) stock is the equivalent of 1 cup (250ml) water plus 1 crumbled stock cube (or 1 teaspoon stock powder). If you prefer to make your own fresh stock, see recipes below.

SUGAR:

We used coarse granulated table sugar, also known as crystal sugar, unless otherwise specified.

Castor: also known as superfine; is fine granulated table sugar.

Icing: also known as confectioners' sugar or powdered sugar. We used icing sugar mixture, not pure icing sugar, unless specified.

TARAMA: salted fish roe.

TOMATO:

Canned: whole peeled tomatoes in natural juices.

Paste: a concentrated tomato puree used in flavouring soups, stews, sauces and casseroles etc.

Puree: is canned, pureed tomatoes (not tomato paste). Use fresh, peeled, pureed tomatoes as a substitute, if preferred.

TRIPE: honeycomb tripe comes from the stomach of an ox. Tripe is sold cleaned, washed and blanched.

VEAL:

Diced: chopped veal

VERMICELLI: thin, clear rice noodles.

VINEGAR:

Brown: malt vinegar.

Cider: vinegar made from fermented apples.

White: made from spirit of cane sugar.

VINE LEAVES: we used vine leaves processed in brine; these are available in jars and packets.

WINE: we used good-quality dry white and red wines.

YEAST: allow 2 teaspoons (7g) dried yeast to each 15g compressed yeast if substituting one for the other.

YOGURT: plain, unflavoured yogurt is used as a meat tenderiser, enricher, thickener and also as a dessert ingredient.

ZUCCHINI: courgette.

MAKE YOUR OWN STOCK

BEEF STOCK

2kg meaty beef bones
2 onions
2 sticks celery, chopped
2 carrots, chopped
3 bay leaves
2 teaspoons black peppercorns
5 litres (20 cups) water
3 litres (12 cups) water, extra

Place bones and unpeeled chopped onions in baking dish. Bake, uncovered, in hot oven about 1 hour or until bones and onions are well browned. Transfer bones and onions to large pan, add celery, carrots, bay leaves, peppercorns and water, simmer, uncovered, 3 hours. Add extra water, simmer, uncovered, further 1 hour; strain.
Makes about 10 cups.
■ Stock can be made 4 days ahead.
■ Storage: Covered, in refrigerator.
■ Freeze: Suitable.
■ Microwave: Not suitable.

CHICKEN STOCK

2kg chicken bones
2 onions, chopped
2 sticks celery, chopped
2 carrots, chopped
3 bay leaves
2 teaspoons black peppercorns
5 litres (20 cups) water

Combine all ingredients in large pan, simmer, uncovered, 2 hours; strain.
Makes about 10 cups.
■ Stock can be made 4 days ahead.
■ Storage: Covered, in refrigerator.
■ Freeze: Suitable.
■ Microwave: Not suitable.

FISH STOCK

1½kg fish bones
3 litres (12 cups) water
1 onion, chopped
2 sticks celery, chopped
2 bay leaves
1 teaspoon black peppercorns

Combine all ingredients in large pan, simmer, uncovered, 20 minutes; strain.
Makes about 10 cups.
■ Stock can be made 4 days ahead.
■ Storage: Covered, in refrigerator.
■ Freeze: Suitable.
■ Microwave: Not suitable.

VEGETABLE STOCK

1 large carrot, chopped
1 large parsnip, chopped
2 onions, chopped
6 sticks celery, chopped
4 bay leaves
2 teaspoons black peppercorns
3 litres (12 cups) water

Combine all ingredients in large pan, simmer, uncovered, 1½ hours; strain.
Makes about 5 cups.
■ Stock can be made 4 days ahead.
■ Storage: Covered, in refrigerator.
■ Freeze: Suitable.
■ Microwave: Not suitable.

INDEX

QUICK CONVERSION GUIDE

Wherever you live in the world, you can use our recipes with the help of our easy-to-follow conversions for all your cooking needs. These conversions are approximate only. The difference between the exact and approximate conversions of liquid and dry measures amounts to only a teaspoon or two, and will not make any noticeable difference to your cooking results.

MEASURING EQUIPMENT

The difference between measuring cups internationally is minimal within 2 or 3 teaspoons' difference. (For the record, 1 Australian metric measuring cup will hold approximately 250ml.) The most accurate way of measuring dry ingredients is to weigh them. When measuring liquids use a clear glass or plastic jug with metric markings.

If you would like metric measuring cups and spoons as used in our Test Kitchen, turn to page 128 for details and order coupon. In this book we use metric measuring cups and spoons approved by Standards Australia.

● a graduated set of 4 cups for measuring dry ingredients; the sizes are marked on the cups.
● a graduated set of 4 spoons for measuring dry and liquid ingredients; the amounts are marked on the spoons.
● 1 TEASPOON: 5ml
● 1 TABLESPOON: 20ml

NOTE: NZ, CANADA, USA AND UK ALL USE 15ml TABLESPOONS.
ALL CUP AND SPOON MEASUREMENTS ARE LEVEL.

DRY MEASURES

METRIC	IMPERIAL
15g	½oz
30g	1oz
60g	2oz
90g	3oz
125g	4oz (¼lb)
155g	5oz
185g	6oz
220g	7oz
250g	8oz (½lb)
280g	9oz
315g	10oz
345g	11oz
375g	12oz (¾lb)
410g	13oz
440g	14oz
470g	15oz
500g	16oz (1lb)
750g	24oz (1½lb)
1kg	32oz (2lb)

LIQUID MEASURES

METRIC	IMPERIAL
30ml	1 fluid oz
60ml	2 fluid oz
100ml	3 fluid oz
125ml	4 fluid oz
150ml	5 fluid oz (¼ pint/1 gill)
190ml	6 fluid oz
250ml	8 fluid oz
300ml	10 fluid oz (½ pint)
500ml	16 fluid oz
600ml	20 fluid oz (1 pint)
1000ml (1 litre)	1¾ pints

WE USE LARGE EGGS
WITH AN AVERAGE
WEIGHT OF 60g

HELPFUL MEASURES

METRIC	IMPERIAL
3mm	⅛in
6mm	¼in
1cm	½in
2cm	¾in
2.5cm	1in
5cm	2in
6cm	2½in
8cm	3in
10cm	4in
13cm	5in
15cm	6in
18cm	7in
20cm	8in
23cm	9in
25cm	10in
28cm	11in
30cm	12in (1ft)

HOW TO MEASURE

When using the graduated metric measuring cups, it is important to shake the dry ingredients loosely into the required cup. Do not tap the cup on the bench, or pack the ingredients into the cup unless otherwise directed. Level top of cup with knife. When using graduated metric measuring spoons, level top of spoon with knife. When measuring liquids in the jug, place jug on flat surface, check for accuracy at eye level.

OVEN TEMPERATURES

These oven temperatures are only a guide; we've given you the lower degree of heat. Always check the manufacturer's manual.

	C˚ (Celsius)	F˚ (Fahrenheit)	Gas Mark
Very slow	120	250	1
Slow	150	300	2
Moderately slow	160	325	3
Moderate	180	350	4
Moderately hot	190	375	5
Hot	200	400	6
Very hot	230	450	7

TWO GREAT OFFERS FROM THE AWW HOME LIBRARY